A THOUSAND WAYS TO YOUR DESTINY

Finding Opportunity In
Inauspicious Spaces

Praise George

Dedicated to everyone who refused to believe that one closed door meant all doors were closed. To everyone who kept knocking. To everyone who found their own way. To everyone who refused to be deterred, who kept moving forward in spite of opposition and adversity. To everyone who dared to believe there are a thousand ways.

Your courage inspires me. Your persistence motivates me. Your success validates the message of this book.

Keep going. Your thousand ways await.

Copyright © 2026 Praise George

All rights reserved

The characters and events portrayed in this book are fictitious. Any similarity to real persons, living or dead, is coincidental and not intended by the author.

No part of this book may be reproduced, or stored in a retrieval system, or transmitted in any form or by any means, electronic, mechanical, photocopying, recording, or otherwise, without express written permission of the publisher.

Disclaimer: The purpose of this book is to provide inspirational insights in navigating your path. It is not meant to replace professional counsel for legal or financial matters, or emotional or psychological issues. Referral to a competent financial adviser or to a qualified counsellor or therapist is recommended for use outside the scope of this publication which is intended for general use and not as a specific course of treatment. Neither the author
nor the publisher take any responsibility for loss occasioned
to any person or organisation acting or refraining from action
as a result of information contained in this publication. All publishing rights belong exclusively to Praise George.
Website: www.youwillbefine.org

ISBN-13: 9781234567890
ISBN-10: 1477123456

Cover design by: Art Painter
Library of Congress Control Number: 2018675309
Printed in the United States of America

INTRODUCTION

YOUR DESTINY HAS NO SINGLE ADDRESS

"For me, I just kept going. I just kept trying. If this is not an inroad for me, I said, 'That's okay, because I'm gonna find another inroad.' If you can't go one way, there are many ways to get where you are going. So you just take a step back and see beyond the wall."

— Cyndi Lauper

I remember sitting in that one-bedroom flat, writing in a notebook, when my landlady walked by. She stopped by my window and regarded me with a question in her eyes. Her question cut through the silence: "What are you doing at home at this hour of the day?"
"I am writing, working on a book," I replied.

She laughed. Not a polite chuckle, but genuine derision. "You are writing? Writing what? Why don't you get a job like everybody else and stop deceiving yourself that you are a writer?"

I was shattered. The old pain resurrected within me, haunting me again. But I summoned the strength to ignore her and kept writing because I had no choice. I was broke. I was desperate. And my only hope for survival was the completion of that book.

That moment crystallized a truth I'd been learning the hard way: there are a thousand ways to your destiny, and most of them look nothing like what society tells you they should.

This book exists because I refused to believe there was only one path to my dreams. When the university system didn't work for me, I left. When traditional employment couldn't contain my vision, I chose entrepreneurship. When people said writers can't make a living in my country, I proved them wrong by selling books in ways no writer had done before.

But here's what I learned: my story isn't exceptional because I'm special. It's simply proof of a principle that applies to every single person reading these words.

There are a thousand ways to your destiny.

Not one way. Not two ways. A thousand ways, and probably more.

WHO THIS BOOK IS FOR

You picked up this book because something inside you knows you're meant for more. Perhaps you're:
- Stuck in a job that drains your soul while everyone tells you to be grateful for stability
- Trapped in a relationship that no longer serves you but paralyzed by the fear of starting over
- Holding onto an opportunity that's clearly dead because you think it's your only chance
- Afraid to pursue your real dream because the path forward isn't clear
- Exhausted from begging people who don't value you for opportunities they'll never give
- Standing at a crossroads, frozen by indecision, wondering which door is the "right" one

If any of these describe you, this book will be your guide. Not because I have all the answers, but because I've learned to ask better questions. Not because I never face closed doors, but because I've learned to find the doors that open.

WHAT YOU'LL DISCOVER

This book is organized into six parts that will take you on a journey from limitation to liberation:
Part One: Breaking Free From Limiting Beliefs

We'll dismantle the lies you've been told about success, failure, and the "right" path. You'll learn why scarcity thinking keeps you begging and how

to walk away from what no longer serves you.
Part Two: Understanding Your Journey

You'll discover how to recognize divine redirection, why companions fall away, and how to trust the unfolding of your unique path—even when it looks nothing like anyone else's.
Part Three: Taking Action On Your Destiny

Theory without action is just philosophy. Here you'll learn how to move forward with uncertainty, knock on the right doors, and find the courage to step into the unknown.
Part Four: Mastering The Inner Game

Success is 80% psychology. We'll address fear, comparison, authenticity, and the internal battles that determine whether you rise or remain stuck.
Part Five: Practical Wisdom For The Journey

From building visibility to following proven mentors, from creating your own luck to knowing when to close doors—these chapters give you actionable strategies for real-world success.
Part Six: A Personal Testimony

I'll share the full story of how I wrote my first book against all odds, and how it opened doors I never knew existed. This is proof that the principles in this book work—because they worked for me.

HOW TO USE THIS BOOK

This isn't a book to read once and forget. It's a manual you'll return to whenever you face a closed door, whenever fear threatens to paralyze you, whenever you need to be reminded that your current path isn't your only option.

Some chapters will hit you harder than others. That's intentional. Read what you need when you need it. Dog-ear the pages that speak to your current situation. Write in the margins. Argue with me. Apply the principles.

At the end of each chapter, you'll find reflection questions and action steps. Don't skip these. The transformation happens not in the reading, but in the doing.

A WORD ABOUT FAITH AND PRACTICALITY

Throughout this book, I reference God, divine guidance, and spiritual principles. This isn't religious posturing—it's honest acknowledgment of what has guided my journey. If faith isn't your framework, translate these concepts into whatever language works for you: the universe, intuition, higher consciousness, life force.

The principles remain the same: there are forces beyond our immediate understanding working in our favor when we align ourselves with growth, authenticity, and courage.

At the same time, this book is intensely practical. Faith without action is delusion. I'll challenge you to knock on doors, build skills, create value, and take responsibility for your outcomes. Destiny isn't passive. It's an active partnership between divine possibility and human effort.

THE PROMISE OF THIS BOOK

I can't promise that reading this book will make you rich, famous, or successful by society's standards. Those outcomes depend on too many variables, including your own effort and choices.

But I can promise this: if you truly absorb the principles in these pages and apply them consistently, you will never again feel trapped by a single closed door. You will never again beg people who don't value you. You will never again believe that one failed opportunity means your dreams are dead.

You'll discover that when one path closes, you have the vision to see alternative routes. When one person rejects you, you'll have the confidence to find someone who recognizes your value. When one method fails, you'll have the creativity to try another approach.

You'll learn to proceed with uncertainty instead of waiting for perfect clarity. You'll develop the courage to walk away from what no longer serves you. You'll build the resilience to keep knocking on doors until the right one opens.

Most importantly, you'll realize that your destiny isn't a single destination at the end of one narrow road. It's a calling that can be fulfilled through countless paths, partnerships, and possibilities.

There are a thousand ways to your destiny. This book will teach you how to find them.

YOUR GREATNESS IS WAITING

Before we begin, I need you to understand something fundamental:

There's greatness in you. You will manifest your greatness. You will live an awesome life—an enviable life, a life worthy of emulation. Greatness is your birthright. That means you were born with all the resources within you that you will require to live a great life.

It doesn't matter where you are on your journey of success. It doesn't matter what challenges you face. It doesn't matter how messed up your life looks at this moment.

Living your greatness is not a matter of if. It is a matter of making a decision to live like you were born to live.

The journey begins with turning the page.

Are you ready?

Before You Begin:

Take a moment right now to write down three

areas of your life where you currently feel stuck, where you believe there's only one way forward and that way is blocked. Be honest. These will be your measuring points as you progress through this book.

1. _____
2. _____
3. _____

By the time you finish this book, you'll see a thousand ways forward for each of these situations. That's not hyperbole. That's the promise of this journey.

Let's begin.

PART ONE: Breaking Free From Limiting Beliefs

1. THE ILLUSION OF ONE PATH

"You must understand that there's more than one way to the top of the mountain."
— Miyamoto Musashi

You've been lied to. Society has sold you the illusion that there is only one path to success, one road to happiness, one way to build a meaningful life. You've been conditioned to believe that if you deviate from the prescribed route—the university degree, the corporate ladder, the acceptable timeline—you've failed.

But this is a prison of thinking, a mental cage that keeps you trapped, desperate, and afraid.

The truth? There are a thousand ways to reach your destination. A thousand routes to your summit. A thousand paths to your purpose.

THE PANIC OF CLOSED DOORS

When one door closes, you panic. When one relationship ends, you think love is over. When one job terminates, you believe your career is finished. When one opportunity slips away, you convince yourself that was your only chance.

But you're wrong. You're operating from the illusion of scarcity, the delusion that life offers you only one shot, one door, one possibility.

This illusion is what makes you beg. It's what makes you grovel at the feet of people who don't deserve your attention. It's what makes you cling to toxic environments, dead-end jobs, and relationships that drain your soul. You stay because you believe there's no other way. You endure abuse because you think this is your only option. You accept mediocrity because you've convinced yourself that this path—this particular path—is the only one that leads anywhere.

Not true.

LIFE IS A MOUNTAIN, NOT A HIGHWAY

Life is not a single highway with one destination. Life is a mountain with countless trails leading to the peak. Some paths are steep and brutal, demanding everything you have. Others wind gently through forests of experience, teaching you lessons you'd never learn on the direct route. Some climbers ascend with aggressive speed. Others move slowly, deliberately, gathering wisdom and strength with each step.

Your path doesn't need to look like anyone else's journey. Your timeline doesn't need to match the timelines of your peers, your family's expectations, or society's arbitrary benchmarks. The mountain doesn't care how you climb it. The summit doesn't judge your route. Success doesn't demand you follow someone else's map.

Look at the entrepreneurs who failed a dozen times before they built empires. Look at the artists who were rejected by every gallery until one said yes. Look at the late bloomers who found their calling at forty, fifty, sixty years old. Look at the people who changed careers entirely and discovered fulfillment they never knew existed.

They all reached their summit. They all made it to the top. But none of them took the same path.

THE PRISON OF LIMITED THINKING

The illusion of one path is what keeps you enslaved. It's what makes you stay in jobs that destroy your spirit because you think this is the only company that can advance your career. It's what makes you remain in cities that suffocate you because you believe opportunity only exists in that location. It's what makes you hold onto friendships that no longer serve you because you think these are the only people who understand you.

This narrow thinking—this belief that there's only one way—is a prison. And you are both the jailer and the prisoner. You've locked yourself into a single possibility, a single vision, a single route. And when that route becomes unbearable, instead of finding another path, you beg. You plead. You diminish yourself. You sacrifice your dignity trying to force a door to stay open when it's time to find another entrance.

ABUNDANCE IS YOUR REALITY

There is abundance in the universe. There are infinite possibilities available to you right now. There are opportunities you haven't even imagined yet. There are doors you haven't noticed because you're too busy staring at the one that closed. There are people you haven't met who will change your life. There are environments you haven't discovered where your talents and skillsets will be celebrated, not tolerated.

But you won't find them if you're stuck in the illusion that there's only one way.

You won't discover new paths if you're clinging desperately to the old one. You won't see the alternative routes if you're on your knees begging someone to let you continue on a road that's clearly wrong for you. You won't recognize better opportunities if you've convinced yourself that this opportunity—the one you're losing—was your only chance.

Your scarcity mentality blinds you. It makes you think small. It makes you settle. It makes you accept crumbs when you deserve a feast. It makes you believe that without this particular person, this particular job, this particular geographical environment, this particular project, this particular situation, you cannot succeed. And that belief becomes a self fulfilling prophecy, it becomes your reality, not because it's true, but because you've made it true through your limited thinking.

THE SIGNS OF THE WRONG PATH

When you're on the wrong path, everything is hard. You have to beg for opportunities. You have to fight for recognition. You have to convince people of your value. You have to push against resistance constantly. You're exhausted, frustrated, unfulfilled. And you think, "This is just how life is. Success requires struggle."

No, it doesn't. What you're experiencing isn't the struggle of growth. It's the friction of being in the wrong place, pursuing the wrong thing, forcing a path that was never yours to walk.

When you're on the right path, things flow. Doors open. Opportunities appear. The right people show up. Your value is recognized naturally. You don't have to beg because what you offer is wanted. You don't have to diminish yourself because the environment values you as you are. Yes, there will be challenges, but they're the kind that make you stronger, not the kind that break your spirit.

If you're constantly having to prove yourself, justify your existence, or beg for scraps of recognition, you're on the wrong path. The mountain has other trails. Find them.

YOUR UNIQUE MAP

There is no single correct route to the top of your mountain. There is no one timeline, no one strategy, no one way to build the life you want. Your journey is yours to design. Your path is yours to create. Your summit is yours to define.

Stop looking at other people's maps. Stop comparing your chapter three to someone else's chapter twenty. Stop believing that because their path worked for them, it must work for you. Stop thinking that because the traditional route didn't work out, you're finished.

You're not finished. You're just getting started on finding your actual path.

Let go of the illusion that there's only one way. Embrace the truth that there are a thousand ways. And if those thousand ways don't work, create the thousand and first way. The mountain is vast. The possibilities are endless. Your potential is limitless. You can find success in inauspicious spaces.

Stop begging to stay on a path that rejects you. Stop clinging to a route that doesn't fit you. Stop forcing yourself into a journey that wasn't designed for who you are.

Find your way. Walk your path. Climb your mountain.

There are a thousand ways to your destiny. Stop acting like there's only one.

REFLECTION QUESTIONS

1. What "one path" have you been clinging to that may actually be limiting you?
2. Where in your life are you begging to stay on a path that clearly isn't working?
3. What alternative routes have you dismissed because they didn't fit the "acceptable" narrative?
4. If there truly were a thousand ways to your goal, what would be three different approaches you could try?

ACTION STEPS

1. Identify your illusion: Write down one area where you believe "this is the only way." Then force yourself to list ten alternative approaches.
2. Research multiple paths: Find three

people who achieved similar goals through completely different methods. Study their journeys.
3. Give yourself permission: Complete this sentence: "I give myself permission to reach my goal without _____."

2. DON'T BE A BEGGAR

"Never stand begging for that which you have the power to earn."

I watched a movie scene that haunts me still. A man was about to be fired from his job. He asked someone to intervene, but they refused. So he took matters into his own hands—but in the worst possible way.

He entered his boss's office and dropped to his knees like a slave, begging for his job. Other staff members watched this display with uncomfortable fascination. You could see the look of disappointment, disgust, and disdain on his boss's face. He looked at him with pity, knowing that he could never allow such a weak, spineless person to remain on his staff.

He fired him anyway.

That man begged for his job because he had a scarcity mentality. He believed that without that job, his life would be screwed. He believed that company was the only place where his career would thrive, where he could advance in life and prosper.

He was wrong.

THE ROOT OF BEGGING: SCARCITY MENTALITY

Scarcity mentality limits you. It's when you fail to realize that there is abundance in the universe, abundance in the world, abundance all around you. Scarcity mentality makes you feel that there is not enough available for you—not enough opportunity, not enough provision, not enough quality relationships, not enough good people to be part of your life, your dream, your journey, your happiness.

Scarcity mentality makes you limit your scope in life. It makes you become parochial in your thinking. You become so narrow-minded that you box yourself into a corner, into a very small corner of the world where nothing good, nothing great, nothing phenomenal, nothing exciting is happening to you.

People beg because they have a scarcity mentality which makes them think they cannot create value to attract the money they need, the relationships they need, the jobs they need, the friendships they need. People beg because they think they are not good enough, smart enough, creative enough, well-connected enough, brilliant enough, educated enough, well-positioned enough on the pyramid of society to create value to get whatever they need.

They think they have to beg other people for those things which have already been given to them: the ability, the skill, the potential to create, to manifest, to attract to themselves what they desire in life.

HOW BEGGING RUINS YOU

Begging makes you subservient to whomever you beg. Begging diminishes you, dehumanizes you, and demeans you.

Don't beg anyone for anything. Don't beg for love, affection, relationship, friendship, or attention. Don't beg for opportunity, help, or advantage.

To think that without having someone or something in your life, you will not be successful or achieve your goals is telling yourself a lie. There are a thousand ways to your destiny. When one door shuts, another door opens. You are never at a loss for what to do or how to proceed on your journey. Never.

All things are working together for your good, for your benefit, and to your advantage. When you understand that all things are working together for your good, you will never demean yourself by begging anyone for anything.

THE WRONG ENVIRONMENT MAKES YOU BEG

When you are in the wrong environment—with the wrong group of people, the wrong person, the wrong organization, the wrong project, the wrong job—you will beg.
Begging humiliates you.
Begging degrades you.
Begging shames you.
Do. Not. Beg.

If you are in an environment where your value is not recognized, received, and rewarded, you are in the wrong environment. If you are in an environment where you are not treated with dignity and respect, you are in the wrong environment. If you are in an environment where you have no peace, you are in the wrong environment.

Instead of demeaning yourself in the wrong environment by kowtowing to people, find the right environment for you and move there.

THE ALTERNATIVE TO BEGGING: VALUE CREATION

Having a scarcity mentality makes you beg idiots who are beneath you for help and opportunity. Having a scarcity mentality makes you kowtow to fools because they are in a position of power. You demean yourself by begging people you are far better than because they seem to be in a position of power, in a position to help you have something, achieve something, or become something.

There's abundance in the universe. There is more than enough available around you for you to prosper and enjoy a good life. Your blessings are not tied to a particular environment, person, group of people, organization, or establishment.

If you are not prospering in an environment, you should move to another environment. Success is impossible in the wrong environment. The wrong environment is where your value is not recognized, rewarded, or appreciated.

The soil in which you're planted matters. You cannot grow in toxic surroundings or in environments that don't foster your growth.

WHAT TO DO INSTEAD

Instead of begging:
1. Create value others cannot ignore. Develop skillsets, knowledge, and expertise that make you indispensable.
2. Position yourself in environments that celebrate your gifts. Move to where your talents are recognized, received and

rewarded.
3. Build self-reliance. Invest in yourself so thoroughly that you become the source of your own opportunities.
4. Develop multiple options. Never be dependent on one person, one company, one opportunity.
5. Walk away with dignity. When an environment doesn't serve you, leave without drama. Your departure is not abandonment—it's liberation.

Remember: you were not born to beg. You were born to create, to contribute, to build value that the world cannot ignore. When you operate from this truth, begging becomes unnecessary and impossible.

REFLECTION QUESTIONS

1. Where in your life are you currently begging for recognition, opportunity, or acceptance?
2. What scarcity beliefs are making you feel like you have no other options?
3. What value could you create that would eliminate the need to beg?
4. What environment needs to change for you to stop feeling like you have to grovel?

ACTION STEPS

1. Identify one situation where you're begging: Write it down honestly. What are you asking for? Who are you asking? Why do you feel you must beg?
2. List your actual value: Write down ten skills, qualities, or forms of value you possess. Reconnect with your worth.
3. Create an exit strategy: For any environment where you're begging, develop a plan to either change your position or leave entirely within 90 days.

3. IF YOU CANNOT WALK AWAY

If you cannot walk away from a person, place, job, business, relationship, or friendship which no longer serves you, which no longer gives you peace, you are a slave to it.
Don't rationalize it.
Don't argue.
Don't give excuses.
Admit it.
You are a slave.

THE DEFINITION OF SLAVERY

If you cannot walk away from something which no longer serves you, which brings you no more value, which gives you no more peace—in fact, it brings you chaos and problems—you have become a slave to that person, place, or thing.
Instead of accepting this truth, some people will

rationalize their inability to walk away, their inability to place their lives in their own hands and determine their own destiny. They will give all kinds of excuses to justify their continuous bondage to that person, place, or thing.

To be a slave means that you have only one option: to be with who you are, to be where you are, and to be doing what you are doing. To be a slave means that you are at the mercy of that person, place, or thing.

True freedom gives you options. If you feel you have no options but to do only one thing in a particular situation, then you've made yourself a victim in that situation. It may be a job, relationship, business, or friendship.

THE COURAGE TEST

To experience true freedom means you can decide and choose whatever direction you want to go with your life. You can walk away from a job, friendship, or relationship which no longer serves you, which has no more relevance in your life. Remaining in a relationship, job, or place because you cannot do without them makes you a slave.

You are a coward if you cannot walk away. You are a coward because you refuse to take responsibility for your life. You refuse to take responsibility for where you are. You refuse to be accountable for the decisions and choices you made and the actions you took which have brought you to where you are.

You are a coward because you refuse to let go of the past and step into what the future holds for you.

THE COST OF STAYING

You will never know what you're capable of achieving if you don't let go of the past and step into the unknown.

You will never release your potential if you remain in an environment, in a job, in a business which has already served its purpose in your life. You will never do more than what you have done. You will never accomplish more than what you have accomplished if you don't let go of the past, let go of the success of the past, let go of your achievement of the past, let go of the great things you have done in the past, and step into the possibilities of the opportunities which exist before you.

THE CATERPILLAR'S CHOICE

Many of us cling to the familiar, even when it no longer serves us. We hold onto the past—relationships that drain us, jobs that stifle us, environments that dim our light—because stepping into the unknown feels daunting.

When something no longer brings you value, peace, or purpose, it has outlived its relevance in your life. Staying tethered to it out of fear transforms you into a prisoner of your own making.

Think of the caterpillar: it must shed its cocoon to become a butterfly. If it clings to the safety of its shell, it never fulfills its destiny. Similarly, you cannot release your potential while remaining in an environment, a job, or a relationship that has already served its purpose.

As C.S. Lewis once said, "There are far, far better things ahead than any we leave behind." The unknown is not a void to fear—it's a canvas of opportunity.

THE POWER OF LETTING GO

Letting go is not a sign of weakness; it is an act of profound strength. It's a declaration that you refuse to be defined by what once was, that you are ready to take responsibility for your life.

Every moment you choose stagnation over growth, you experience a small death—a death of potential, of possibility, of the person you could become. The valiant, however, embrace the inevitable uncertainties of life, trusting that even in the face of fear, the future holds something greater.

William Shakespeare captured this truth perfectly: "Cowards die many times before their deaths; the valiant never taste of death but once. Of all the wonders that I yet have heard it seems to me most strange that men should fear; seeing that death, a necessary end, will come when it will come."

Choose valor over cowardice. Release the weight of

yesterday and embrace the promise of tomorrow. Fear is inevitable, but cowardice is a choice.

Step into the unknown, and let the world witness the extraordinary things you're capable of achieving. The future is yours—claim it.

REFLECTION QUESTIONS

1. What situation in your life are you unable to walk away from, even though it no longer serves you?
2. What are you truly afraid of if you leave? (Be brutally honest.)
3. What is staying in this situation costing you in terms of potential, peace, and possibility?
4. What would the bravest version of you do right now?

ACTION STEPS

1. Name your prison: Write down the one situation where you feel enslaved. Don't sugarcoat it.
2. Calculate the real cost: Make two columns —one for what you gain by staying, one for what it costs you. Be thorough.
3. Design your escape route: Even if you're not ready to leave today, create a detailed plan for how you *could* leave if you chose to. Having a plan reduces fear.

4. Take one brave step: Do one small thing this week that asserts your freedom—even if it's just speaking up, setting a boundary, or researching alternatives.

4. FATALISM AND SUCCESS

"Fatalism is the lazy man's way of accepting the inevitable."- Natalie Clifford Barney

Some people are fatalistic. They believe "if it is mine, it will come to me." They believe that "what will be will be." They believe that the stars determine their future. They believe that if God wants them to have something, then it will happen for them.
This is fatalistic thinking.
It is absolute nonsense.

THE TRAP OF PASSIVE WAITING

What will be is what you make happen by and for yourself. If you desire any good thing in life, you have to pursue it, go after it, invest in it, and make it happen.

Good things don't come to those who wait. In fact, those who wait get absolutely nothing. If you desire something, don't wait for it. Go for it. Make it happen.

Many people have missed great opportunities in life because they believed that if it was theirs, then it would come to them or happen for them. They missed opportunities for high-value relationships because they foolishly expected those relationships to "happen organically." They missed opportunities to make lots of money because they waited for the opportunity to "work out for them." They missed out on having high-value romantic partners because they expected that if that partner belonged in their life, they wouldn't need to work on and maintain their relationship.

This is the seductive lie of fatalism: that destiny is something that happens *to* you rather than something you actively create.

THE GARDEN PRINCIPLE

My wife does some gardening behind our house. She has tomatoes, peppers, apples, and more. The only thing that grows in that garden without work is weeds. If you leave the plants to grow by themselves, they will soon be overwhelmed by weeds. She intentionally protects the plants by weeding her garden, and this helps the plants grow and flourish.

This is the truth about life: the good things require cultivation. The things of value require intention, effort, and consistent care. Only the weeds—the problems, the distractions, the obstacles—grow without effort.

If you want something good to happen in your life, you have to make it happen. You have to invest ime, effort and resources to create, birth it and make it happen. Good things don't happen by themselves. We make them happen with singular focus, intentionality and by taking massive action.

THE ILLUSION OF "MEANT TO BE"

Fatalism is particularly dangerous because it sounds spiritual. It sounds wise. It sounds like faith. "If God wants it for me, it will happen." "What's meant to be will be." "The universe will provide."

But this confuses trust with passivity. True faith is active. It's the belief that when you do your part, divine forces will support you. It's not the abdication of responsibility disguised as surrender.

Consider the farmer who plants seeds and then says, "If God wants me to have a harvest, it will grow." But he never waters the field, never removes the weeds, never protects the crops from pests.

When harvest time comes and there's nothing to gather, is it because God didn't want him to prosper? Or is it because he confused faith with laziness?

God gives you opportunities, talents, and possibilities. But He expects you to cultivate them. The universe presents doorways, but you must walk through them. Destiny is a co-creation, not a passive reception.

THE COST OF WAITING

The most heartbreaking aspect of fatalistic thinking is watching people's dreams die while they wait for life to deliver those dreams to their doorstep.

I've seen talented people wait for recognition instead of promoting their work. I've seen entrepreneurs wait for investors to discover them instead of pitching their ideas. I've seen writers wait for publishers to notice them instead of self-publishing. I've seen singles wait for "the one" to magically appear instead of actively creating opportunities to meet compatible people.

And while they wait, life moves on. Opportunities go to those who pursue them. Recognition goes to those who make themselves visible. Success goes to those who take action.

Time doesn't pause for your fatalism. The world doesn't stop spinning while you wait for fate to intervene.

FROM FATALISM TO INTENTIONALITY

The antidote to fatalism is intentionality—the deliberate choice to pursue what you desire with focus, effort, and persistence.

Intentionality means:
- Setting clear goals instead of vague wishes
- Taking daily action instead of waiting for "someday"
- Creating opportunities instead of hoping they appear
- Building skills instead of expecting natural talent to be enough
- Networking actively instead of waiting to be discovered
- Learning from failures instead of seeing them as signs you weren't "meant" to succeed

When you shift from fatalism to intentionality, you reclaim your power. You stop being a passive recipient of whatever life randomly delivers and become an active architect of your destiny.

THE BALANCE

This doesn't mean you should try to control everything or ignore the role of grace, serendipity, providence, or favorable circumstances in success. There are elements beyond your control. There are moments when doors open that you didn't even know existed. There are times when the right person appears at exactly the right moment.

But here's the key: these moments of grace tend to appear for those who are already in motion. Opportunities find those who are actively pursuing their goals. Luck favors those who show up consistently. Divine intervention supports those who are already doing their part.

You don't have to choose between faith and action. You need both. Trust the process, but work the process. Believe in divine timing, but don't use it as an excuse for procrastination. Surrender outcomes, but never surrender effort.

YOUR PART TO PLAY

There's a powerful prayer that captures this balance: "God grant me the serenity to accept the things I cannot change, courage to change the things I can, and wisdom to know the difference."

Fatalism collapses everything into the first category—accepting everything as unchangeable. But most of what happens in your life falls into the second category: things you absolutely can change through deliberate action.

Your health? You can change that with better habits.

Your skills? You can change that with consistent practice.

Your network? You can change that by reaching out to people.

Your financial situation? You can change that by creating value and managing money wisely.

Your knowledge? You can change that by reading, learning, and studying.

These aren't things to wait for. These are things to actively pursue.

REFLECTION QUESTIONS

1. Where in your life have you been waiting for things to "just happen" instead of making them happen?
2. What opportunities have you missed because you believed "if it's meant to be, it will be"?
3. What would change if you took full responsibility for pursuing what you desire?
4. What's one goal you've been passive about that requires active pursuit?

ACTION STEPS

1. Identify your fatalistic beliefs: Write down three areas where you've been waiting instead of acting. Be honest about the "spiritual" excuses you've been using.
2. Create an action plan: For each area, list three concrete actions you could take this week to actively pursue what you want.
3. Plant your garden: Choose one goal and

treat it like a garden. What needs to be planted? What needs to be watered? What weeds need to be removed? Then do the work.
4. Track your effort: For the next 30 days, journal your daily actions toward your goal. At the end, you'll see clearly whether your results came from fate or from your effort.

5. LIFE AND SCHOOL ARE NOT THE SAME

School punishes failure.
Life demands failure as a prerequisite for success.
School and Life are not the same.

THE SCHOOL CONDITIONING

School punishes failure. School shames you for failure. School embarrasses you for failure. School makes you feel useless and worthless because of failure. Lecturers threatened us with failure in university. A particular lecturer started his lecture by saying, "You will fail this course." The threat of failure was a weapon he wielded over us. It hung over our minds like a guillotine. We felt like French nobility kneeling with the blade hanging over our heads, waiting for execution.

We were terrified of failure as if it were a criminal

offense, as if we would be condemned to a life of shame and suffering if we failed. School instilled the fear of failure in us so much that we were scared to argue with our lecturers or speak freely about our own ideas.

School made us slaves because of fear.

School told us that if we failed in school, we were destined to fail and become useless in life.

But school was wrong.

LIFE'S DIFFERENT LESSON

'Failure is data.' Elon Musk.

Life taught me a different lesson.

Life encourages failure. In fact, life demands failure as a necessary prerequisite for success. In life, failure is the fertilizer for success. Failure accelerates your journey toward success. There are lessons you learn from failure that you can learn no other way. Failure is one of the best teachers in life.

Life encourages failure because success in life is an outcome of trial and error. To be successful, you have to try new things you've never done, go to places you've never been, talk to people you've never met, ask strangers for support, collaboration, and assistance. In life, you have to present your ideas to people who will reject you over and over again until you meet someone who recognizes, receives, and is willing to reward your value.

REGURGITATION VS. INNOVATION

School encourages you to regurgitate what you were taught in class, but life demands that you experiment, explore new ways of thinking, new ways of approaching and solving problems. School didn't give you the option to think for yourself or solve problems for yourself. You always depended on what your lecturers taught you. In fact, you were punished if you said something different from what your lecturer taught in class.

In school, the proof of intelligence was the regurgitation of the same old ideas and concepts to pass an exam. In life, the proof of intelligence is the ability to solve problems life throws at you, the ability to create value, the ability to live life on your own terms.

Life encourages you to explore new ideas and possibilities. It encourages engaging in experiments to create value and invent new products. Failure is a gift. If it weren't for the gift of failure, we wouldn't have the light bulb.

THE ELON MUSK PRINCIPLE

Elon Musk said failure is data. What does this mean?

Each time SpaceX sends up Starship it spends

$100m.

Each time Starship failed its test, it wasn't $100m wasted. It was collection of valuable data they wouldn't have had if they never spent that $100m.

Failure = Data = Iteration = Improvement = Success.

Therefore, failure is a necessary requirement for success.

THE EDISON PRINCIPLE

The inventor Thomas Edison conducted experiments and failed over a thousand times before he discovered the filament for the light bulb. With each failure, he came closer to discovering the solution to the challenge before him. After a thousand failures, he finally succeeded and invented the incandescent light bulb.

If Thomas Edison had been in school, he would have been called an irredeemable failure, a total waste, and expelled. How could you have failed the same course over a thousand times? It would be unforgivable. He would have been punished, shamed, and disgraced for it.

But life and school are not the same. Life encouraged his failures. Life celebrated each step he took toward the discovery of a new product. At the end of his life, Thomas Edison held 1,093 patents. His most famous inventions include the phonograph, the incandescent light bulb, and the motion picture camera. For each of these products, he conducted thousands of experiments, and 99% of them were failures. But he was undeterred and forged ahead until he achieved a breakthrough.

Edison famously said, "I have not failed. I've just found 10,000 ways that won't work." This is the mindset life rewards—the mindset school punishes.

THE CONDITIONING WE MUST BREAK

School conditioned us to be afraid of failure, afraid of trying something new, something we've never done, because we could fail and failure is taboo. This is the reason why many of you have good degrees but have been conditioned by school not to dare things you've never done. So you keep job hunting instead of using your educated brain to create solutions to your problems.

Your degree means absolutely nothing in real life if you cannot use it in value creation to solve your problems. To be successful in life, you have to go against the fear of failure and dare to deploy your talents, skillsets, and expertise in value creation.

WHAT LIFE ACTUALLY REWARDS

In the real world:
Failure means you're learning. Every failed

attempt teaches you what doesn't work, bringing you closer to what does.

Failure means you're trying. The only people who never fail are those who never attempt anything meaningful.

Failure means you're growing. Growth happens at the edge of your comfort zone, where failure is inevitable.

Failure means you're alive. A life without failure is a life without ambition, risk, or courage.

The most successful people in the world are those who failed the most—and kept going. Every billionaire has multiple failed ventures. Every successful author has a drawer full of rejected manuscripts. Every accomplished athlete has suffered defeats. Every innovator has prototypes that didn't work.

The difference between those who succeed and those who don't isn't the presence or absence of failure. It's the willingness to fail, learn, adjust, and try again.

UNLEARNING THE SCHOOL MENTALITY

If you want to succeed in life, you must consciously unlearn what school taught you about failure:

School taught: Failure is shameful.
Life teaches: Failure is educational.
School taught: Get it right the first time.

Life teaches: Iterate until it works.
School taught: Follow the prescribed method.
Life teaches: Innovate your own approach.
School taught: The teacher has all the answers.
Life teaches: You must find your own solutions.
School taught: One wrong answer means you fail.
Life teaches: Multiple wrong attempts lead to the right answer.
School taught: Stay in your lane and don't challenge authority.
Life teaches: Challenge assumptions and create your own path.

YOUR REAL EDUCATION BEGINS NOW

Your formal education ended when you left school. Your real education—the one that determines your actual success—begins when you embrace failure as part of the learning process.

Start that business even if it might fail. Write that book even if it might be rejected. Ask for that opportunity even if they might say no. Try that new approach even if it might not work. Pitch that idea even if they might laugh.

Every failure is tuition paid toward your eventual success. The question is: are you willing to pay it?

REFLECTION QUESTIONS

1. How has school's punishment of failure

affected your willingness to take risks?
2. What have you not attempted because you're afraid of failing?
3. What could you learn from a failure that you can't learn from always playing it safe?
4. If failure were guaranteed not to kill you or harm you permanently, what would you try?

ACTION STEPS

1. Reframe past failures: List three "failures" from your past. For each one, write down three things you learned from that experience.
2. Attempt something with high failure risk: This week, try something where failure is likely. It could be as simple as attempting a recipe you've never made, asking for a discount, or pitching an idea. The goal is to practice failing without catastrophe.
3. Study successful failures: Research three successful people in your field. Document their failures before their breakthrough. Let their journeys normalize failure for you.
4. Create a "Failure Resume": Write down all your significant failures and what each one taught you. You'll see your failures are actually your credentials.

END OF PART ONE

You've now broken free from the most limiting beliefs that keep people stuck: the illusion that there's only one path, the habit of begging instead of creating value, the fear of walking away from what no longer serves you, the passivity of fatalism, and the crippling fear of failure.

In Part Two, we'll explore how to understand and navigate your unique journey to destiny.

PART TWO: UNDERSTANDING YOUR JOURNEY

6. WALK YOUR OWN PATH

From childhood, we all have been taught to conform to the expectations of our parents, teachers, and authority figures. We are forced to conform to peer pressure in school and in the workplace. You want to be like your friends, buy what they buy, attend the same parties and events, join the same social clubs, identify with them in as many ways as possible. However, there comes a time in our lives when we have to choose our own path and move in a direction that best represents our dream, that best serves our interests and propagates our agenda.

THE FORCED CHOICE

There comes a time when we either grow up and decide for ourselves what is best for us, or we allow the vicissitudes of life to force us to move in a direction which we never planned for—and sometimes a direction which we were not even prepared for. We are confronted with a difficult situation, and the only option that makes sense to us is to choose our own path and move away from the paths that our friends, peers, and colleagues have chosen.

Whether you like it or not, whether you believe it or not, the day will come that you must make a decision and choose a path for yourself. Not one chosen by your parents, friends, spouse, or mentors. As hard as it may be, the burden will fall squarely on your shoulders, and you will be compelled to walk boldly on your own path, to pursue your own dream, to live your own life on your own terms.

THE MACHINERY OF CONFORMITY

Everything around us wants us to conform. Social media is a tool of propaganda and lies designed to indoctrinate you to conform to the biases, beliefs, and agenda of powerful people who control those platforms and those who have the resources to grab your attention by boosting their posts with paid ads.

Nothing on social media is as it seems. I watched a documentary in which Saudi Arabia pays thousands of people to post tweets in defense of its policies. That was when I discovered that anything trending on social media is sponsored by someone who has an agenda. There are news items that are silenced by people with an agenda, and there are news items that are blown out of proportion to become instruments of propaganda and indoctrination.

If you don't want to follow the mindless crowd, you must learn to think for yourself, scrutinize every piece of information you see online, choose what to believe, and walk your own path in life.

THE COST OF CONFORMITY

When you conform, you trade your unique value for acceptance. You trade your authentic voice for approval. You trade your distinct vision for belonging. And what do you get in return? The temporary comfort of fitting in with people who wouldn't recognize your true self if they met it.

Conformity feels safe because it's familiar, predictable, and supported by the masses. But it's a slow death of everything that makes you uniquely you. Your gifts, your perspectives, your unconventional approaches—these are precisely what the world needs from you, but conformity requires you to suppress them.

Consider this: every major innovation, every breakthrough, every transformation in human history came from someone who refused to conform. They walked their own path despite ridicule, rejection, and resistance.

THE COURAGE TO DIVERGE

Walking your own path doesn't mean being contrarian for the sake of being different. It means:
Following your internal compass, not the crowd's GPS. Your intuition knows your path better than anyone else's opinion.

Making choices aligned with your values, not society's expectations. Your life should reflect what you believe, not what they demand.

Pursuing opportunities that call to you, even if they seem unconventional. The road less traveled exists because it's harder—but often leads somewhere better.

Thinking independently rather than absorbing groupthink. Question assumptions. Challenge narratives. Form your own conclusions.

Being willing to be misunderstood. When you walk your own path, people who follow the main road will think you're lost. Let them think it.

THE LONELINESS AND LIBERATION

Walking your own path means accepting that you will sometimes walk alone. Your friends who took the conventional route will question your choices. Your family may worry you're making mistakes. Society may judge you as reckless or foolish.

But there's profound liberation in choosing your own way. You're no longer performing for an audience. You're no longer contorting yourself to fit into boxes designed for someone else. You're no longer sacrificing your dreams on the altar of other people's comfort.

The loneliness is temporary. Eventually, you'll meet other path-walkers—people who also had the courage to choose their own direction. These become your true tribe: not people you conform with, but people you co-create with.

YOUR PATH IS VALID

You don't need permission to walk your own path. You don't need consensus. You don't need everyone to understand or approve.

Your path is valid because it's yours. Your timing is valid because it's yours. Your methods are valid because they're yours.

Stop waiting for validation from people who are themselves waiting for validation. Stop seeking approval from people who sacrificed their own dreams for acceptance.

Start trusting yourself. Start honoring your inner knowing. Start moving in the direction that resonates with your soul, even if it makes zero sense to everyone else.

REFLECTION QUESTIONS

1. In what areas of your life are you conforming to others' expectations rather than following your own path?
2. What would you do differently if you

weren't worried about what people think?
3. Who in your life do you admire specifically because they walk their own path?
4. What's one decision you need to make based on your values rather than others' expectations?

ACTION STEPS

1. Identify your conformity: List three ways you're currently conforming to fit in. Be brutally honest.
2. Define your true path: Write a vision for your life based solely on your values, interests, and calling—ignore what "should" be included.
3. Make one divergent choice: This week, make one decision that aligns with your authentic path, even if it's unconventional.
4. Find your tribe: Seek out one community, group, or individual who celebrates non-conformity and authentic paths.

7. YOUR LIFE IS MORE THAN WHERE YOU ARE

Years ago, I worked in a trading company. I told my boss that I wanted to write books. He looked at me with doubt on his face and said: "You cannot write books. What do you know about writing books?"

His words were discouraging, but I refused to give up. I held on to my dream and wrote my first book, self-published it, and that book changed my life.

THE LIMITING BELIEF

You are more than where you are. You are more than what you do in life. You can do more with your life.

The reason why some people are stagnated or stuck in one company, one business, one job, or one geographical environment is because they think that job, business, company, or geographical environment is what defines and determines their life and their future. They think that without doing what they do, without being at that job, in that business, in that environment, they will not be successful—they will live a substandard life.

It is delusional to think that without working in a particular company your life is going to be useless or you will become a failure, or that without being part of a particular business your life will be meaningless. That is utter nonsense.

YOUR LIFE IS PORTABLE

Your life, your future, is not tied to a particular place, job, business, person, group of people, or environment. It is because you think that without a particular job, business, environment, or relationship you will not be successful that you hold on to things which are of no value to you, things which have served their purpose in your life, things which have no more relevance in your life, things which you have outgrown, which you ought to walk away from.

Your talents transfer. Your skills are portable. Your value is inherent to you, not to your location. You can create, contribute, and succeed in countless environments, industries, and situations.

Richard Branson said, "Business opportunities are like buses, there's always one coming around." Your life is not defined by one opportunity, one job, or one geographical environment. You can blossom and prosper elsewhere, doing something else.

THE FEAR THAT BINDS

It is fear of the unknown which makes you hold on to things which have outlived their usefulness in your life, things which bring you no value. Fear makes you stay where you ought to have left, makes you live in an environment which no longer serves you in any way, makes you attach yourself to people and relationships who no longer make any valuable contribution to your life.

It is fear that makes you stay in a place which you ought to have left, hold on to a relationship which you ought to have let go, stay in a job or business which you ought to have walked away from. And while you are holding on to these things in fear, opportunities pass you by, life passes you by, open doors pass you by, possibilities pass you by, great relationships pass you by.

BREAKING THE GEOGRAPHICAL TRAP

To make real progress in life, you have to let go of the mentality that makes you think that your future is tied to one place, one thing, one opportunity. It is a scarcity mentality, and it will keep you limited. You will never maximize your potential if you continue to think like that.

Many people stay in cities that offer them no opportunities because they're familiar. They remain in regions that don't value their gifts because "this is home." They cling to locations that limit their growth because they fear the unknown of somewhere new.

But your greatness isn't location-specific. Your destiny isn't tied to GPS coordinates. The right environment for your flourishing might be across the city, across the country, or across the world.

THE IDENTITY BEYOND TITLE

You are not your job title. You are not your company's org chart. You are not your industry. You are not your current business model.

You are a collection of transferable value: skills, wisdom, creativity, work ethic, problem-solving ability, relationship-building capacity, and unique perspectives. These things go with you wherever you go. They adapt to new contexts. They create value in multiple markets.

When you identify too closely with where you are or what you currently do, you limit your ability to see where else you could go and what else you could do. You've confused your current expression with your total capacity.

THE COURAGE TO RELOCATE

Sometimes your breakthrough requires relocation —not just geographical, but professional, social, and psychological.

Professional relocation: Changing industries, roles, or career trajectories entirely.

Social relocation: Moving into new circles, networks, and communities that match your growth.

Psychological relocation: Shifting your self-concept from who you've been to who you're becoming.

Geographical relocation: Physically moving to places where opportunity matches your ambition.

Each of these requires courage because it means leaving behind the familiar for the uncertain. But the familiar is often just another word for stagnant.

BLOOM WHERE YOU'RE REPLANTED

You've heard "bloom where you're planted." That's good advice for contentment. But sometimes you need to bloom where you're *re*planted. Sometimes the soil you're in is depleted. Sometimes the climate where you are doesn't suit your species. Sometimes you need to transplant yourself to an environment where you can actually thrive.

This isn't about running away from challenges or avoiding hard work. This is about recognizing when a situation has become genuinely limiting rather than temporarily challenging.

Break the hold of fear over your mind by taking

action on your dream to do more with your life and achieve more with your skillsets, talents, and abilities. You've got a brilliant mind—don't let it go to waste by confining yourself to one place, one person, and one geographical environment.

REFLECTION QUESTIONS

1. What environment, job, or location are you staying in primarily out of fear rather than genuine opportunity?
2. How would your life change if you gave yourself permission to relocate (professionally, geographically, or socially)?
3. What skills and value do you possess that would transfer to completely different contexts?
4. If fear weren't a factor, where would you go and what would you do?

ACTION STEPS

1. Assess your environment: Rate your current environment (job, location, social circle) on a scale of 1-10 for how well it supports your growth. Be honest.
2. Research alternatives: Spend 2 hours researching three completely different environments (cities, industries, companies) where people with your skills

thrive.
3. Build portability: Identify your three most valuable transferable skills. How could these create value in a different context?
4. Take one relocating action: Make one move this week that represents relocation —apply for a job in a different field, attend an event in a new community, or research moving to a different city.

8. WHEN GOD WANTS TO CHANGE YOUR LIFE

There are moments in life when you feel stuck, confused, or lost. You may wonder why certain things aren't working out, why doors are closing, or why certain people seem to drift away from you. These moments often signify that God is preparing to make a significant shift in your life.

When God wants to change your life for the better, His divine hand moves in specific ways, orchestrating events that may not make sense at first but are part of His perfect plan. Here are seven things that happen when God is positioning you for transformation.

1. GOD REMOVES YOU FROM THE WRONG ENVIRONMENT

Success is impossible in the wrong environment. The wrong environment is where your value is not recognized, rewarded, or appreciated. It's the place where you feel drained, where your potential is stifled, and where you cannot thrive. Sometimes, God will close doors to familiar spaces, relationships, or job opportunities to lead you out of an environment that no longer serves your purpose.

The soil in which you're planted matters. You cannot grow in toxic surroundings or in environments that don't foster your growth. You will be inspired to move to a place where your gifts, talents, and value will be recognized, received, and rewarded.

Trust the process. Even if it feels uncomfortable, know that God is moving you out of a place that no longer aligns with your destiny. Let go and prepare for the next season of your life and journey.

2. GOD REMOVES THE WRONG PEOPLE FROM YOUR LIFE

The people we surround ourselves with have a profound impact on our journey. The wrong people do not recognize, receive, or reward your value. They may drain your energy, discourage your dreams, or prevent you from growing. When God wants to elevate you, He often removes individuals who no longer serve your purpose or who might hinder your progress.

Not everyone can go where you are headed. The wrong people can delay or derail your destiny. God wants to surround you with those who will uplift, encourage, and align with His purpose for your life.

It's natural to feel pain when some people leave, but trust God. The removal of wrong people creates space for the right ones to enter your life—people who will honor and uplift your value.

3. GOD SHUTS SOME DOORS

It's easy to feel disheartened when opportunities seem to slip through your fingers or when certain paths are suddenly blocked. However, when God shuts a door, it's because He's redirecting you to something better. Not every opportunity is meant for you, and some doors must be closed for you to move forward.

Closed doors are God's protection. He knows what's ahead, and sometimes, the very thing you're pursuing could lead to harm or delay in your destiny. Shutting certain doors helps you avoid unnecessary detours and distractions.

Instead of feeling discouraged, see closed doors as a sign that God is moving you in a new, better direction. Trust that every "no" is guiding you toward a more significant "yes."

4. GOD OPENS NEW DOORS BEFORE YOU

When one door closes, another door opens. There are no lost opportunities in the kingdom. When one door shuts, another door opens that aligns better with your purpose. These new doors represent new opportunities, connections, or pathways that lead to your growth and success. God wants to position you for the best opportunities that align with His plan for your life. New doors represent new seasons, new growth, and new possibilities.

Be open to exploring new opportunities, even if they feel unfamiliar or outside of your comfort zone. Trust that you are being led to places where you will flourish and where your value will be recognized, received, and rewarded.

5. GOD GIVES YOU IDEAS TO CREATE COMPELLING VALUE

In times of transition, God often plants seeds of creativity and inspiration within you. He gives you new ideas, solutions, and visions that enable you to create and deliver value. Whether it's a business idea, a ministry, or a personal project, God equips you to contribute meaningfully to the world around you.

God wants you to prosper, and prosperity comes through value creation. He will give you the insight and creativity to solve problems, meet needs, and add value to others' lives. Your success will flow from the value you create.

Pay attention to the ideas and inspirations that come your way. Write them down, pray over them, and start taking small steps toward bringing them to life. God is equipping you for greater things.

6. GOD GRANTS YOU FAVOR WITH RANDOM PEOPLE AND STRANGERS

One of the most incredible signs of divine favor is when random people, even strangers, go out of their way to help you, expecting nothing in return. These people may offer opportunities, resources, or connections that propel you forward in ways you couldn't have orchestrated on your own. This is God working behind the scenes, opening doors and creating divine appointments.

God uses people as vessels to fulfill His will in your life. Favor with strangers is a sign of His hand upon you, moving in unexpected ways to bless and guide you toward your purpose.

Be open to the help and kindness of others. Recognize that God often works through people to bring about His plans in your life. Stay grateful and humble as these blessings unfold.

7. GOD GIVES YOU SPECIFIC INSTRUCTIONS

When God wants to change your life, you often receive clear instructions—to go somewhere, meet someone, or take a specific action. These instructions are designed to position you for the next season of your life. It may seem like a small step, but it can lead to significant breakthroughs.

God's instructions align us with a divine agenda. He gives us clear direction to ensure we are in the right place at the right time, meeting the right people, and taking the right actions. His instructions are always for our benefit and His glory.

Listen closely for divine inspiration. It may come through prayer, scripture, or even a feeling of conviction in your heart. Once you receive His instruction, act on it with faith, knowing that obedience opens the door to His blessings.

THE PROMISE OF TRANSFORMATION

When God wants to change your life for good, He orchestrates events that may not always make sense at first. But as He removes the wrong people, opens new doors, grants you favor, and gives you specific instructions, trust that every step is leading you toward a life of greater purpose, peace, and fulfillment.

God's plan for your life is always better than anything you could imagine—stay open, stay obedient, and watch the transformation unfold.

For more information read my book: Finding Direction.

REFLECTION QUESTIONS

1. What environment or relationship has God been trying to remove you from?
2. What closed door have you been mourning instead of trusting?
3. What new ideas or inspirations have you been ignoring or dismissing?
4. What specific instruction might God be giving you that you've been afraid to follow?

ACTION STEPS

1. Identify divine removals: List the people or situations God has removed from your life in the past year. With hindsight, can you see why?
2. Notice new doors: Write down three new opportunities that have appeared recently. Even if they seem small or strange, write them down.
3. Act on inspiration: Choose one idea or instruction you've received recently and

take one concrete action on it this week.
4. Practice divine awareness: For the next week, pay attention to "random" favor, unexpected help, or strange coincidences. Write them down and look for patterns.

END OF PART TWO

You now understand that your journey has multiple paths, that companions will come and go, that you must walk your own unique route, that you're not limited by your current location, and that God orchestrates changes that might initially feel like losses but are actually redirections toward your destiny.

In Part Three, we'll shift from understanding to action—learning how to actively pursue your destiny with courage, strategy, and unwavering commitment.

9. A THOUSAND WAYS TO YOUR DESTINY

There are a thousand ways for you to get to your destiny. By destiny, I mean the fulfillment of your dream, calling, or assignment.

You may think that it is your degree that will take you to your destiny, or your skillset, or your wealthy family, or your present job position, or your business, or your present relationships—and you may be completely wrong. God may have a better plan to manifest your dream through you.

THE DANGER OF SINGLE-PATH THINKING

It is because people think that there is one path, one person, one possibility to the fulfillment of their dream that they become stagnated, stuck on one spot, with one person or opportunity, doing the same thing for years and going nowhere. They become slaves to a particular situation, and their dream becomes grounded.

Many people were tied to a particular person or path they thought would take them to greatness, but they were disappointed. They were so disillusioned that they buried their dreams and settled for a life of mediocrity.

But instead of giving up on your dream, you should understand that there are a thousand ways to your destiny.

There are a thousand paths.

There are a thousand doors.

There are a thousand helpers.

There are a thousand windows.

There are a thousand possibilities.

There are a thousand opportunities.

There are a thousand possible permutations to bring you to your destiny.

WHEN ONE DOOR CLOSES

When one door closes, another door will open. When one path is blocked, another path will open up to you. When one person disappoints you, another helper will show up for you. When one opportunity is missed, another opportunity is presented to you.

God is not limited to one person, one place, one opportunity, one position, one nation, one job, one business, one relationship, etc, to get you to your place of destiny. God keeps working in and with the circumstances and vicissitudes of life to create new possibilities and empower you to scale all obstacles to arrive at your destiny.

It is impossible for you to be stranded, stagnated, or stopped. Before new challenges arise in your life, God has already made a way for you to triumph. Romans 8:28 says: "And we know that God causes all things to work together for good to those who love God, to those who are called according to His purpose."

THE DIVINE APPOINTMENTS

On your journey, people will enter your life for a divine assignment, and when they have served their purpose, they will exit your life. People may enter your life for five hours, five days, five months, or five years. You should never confuse someone with a five-hour assignment in your life with someone who has a five-year strategic relationship with you. They are on different levels of relevance and should be treated accordingly.

People with whom you are in a strategic relationship may fail you due to circumstances beyond their control. An opportunity may fall through. But God will never fail you. As much as good relationships are critical for success, we must never forget that people can fail us when we put our trust in them. We should be grateful for every strategic relationship the Lord brings into our lives, but we must never forget that it is God who is the one behind these relationships and opportunities.

THE IDOL TRAP

When we fail to acknowledge God and give Him His rightful place in our lives, we will turn people into idols, place them on a pedestal on which they don't belong, and pour on them the accolades that should only be given to God.

Some people turn their helpers into demi-gods and become their slaves, completely forgetting that it was God who sent them those helpers. They cower before such people and do anything they tell them to do in order to gain more favor with them.

No person should be worshiped like an idol. God sends people into our lives to effect His divine agenda, not to make them lords over us. When we take our eyes away from God and place them on people, God quickly corrects that situation by separating us from such people.

GOD'S SUPERNATURAL WAYS

God has a thousand ways to bring us to the place of our destiny. He will make a way where there is no way. He will open impossible doors. He will bring oil out of a rock. He will make a way in the wilderness. He will make a way in the oceans. He will open pathways of advancement in difficult places. He will bring about supernatural provisions. He will cause blessings to rain on you in the most unusual ways and in inauspicious spaces.

God knows how to detangle and disengage our lives from chaotic, difficult situations and relationships, bring us out, and strategically position us for greatness.

God knows how to take Joseph through the caravan of the Ishmaelites and bring him into Egypt where he would be positioned in the house of Potiphar to begin his journey into greatness.

God knows how to position Moses to be noticed and picked up by Pharaoh's daughter, to be raised in the palace of his enemies as a prince of Egypt.

God knows how to bring Esther into the palace for a beauty competition, through a random selection, to be chosen by the king to be his wife, and to be in a position to deliver the Jews from the holocaust and extermination planned by the racist and wicked Haman, who fell into the pit he had prepared for God's people.

THE RESPONSE TO CLOSED DOORS

Instead of weeping at the doorstep of an opportunity that has slipped through your fingers, or a relationship that has fizzled out, or a business that has collapsed, or a job from which you have been fired, lift up your eyes to the Lord and realize that God has a thousand ways to bring you to your destiny.

Even though some doors may be shut against you or some opportunities lost, God will open new doors, create new opportunities, and connect you with brilliant people in strategic relationships to help bring you to your destiny and the fulfillment of your dream.

THE PRACTICAL REALITY

This isn't just spiritual theory. This is lived reality. I've experienced it in my own life. When one publishing path closed, self-publishing opened. When one income stream dried up, three others emerged. When certain relationships ended, better ones formed. When one ministry opportunity vanished, a broader platform appeared.

Every single time I thought, "This is the only way," life showed me I was wrong. And not just wrong—I was limiting God's creativity in manifesting my destiny.

The key is to hold your dreams tightly while holding your methods loosely. Be absolutely committed to your calling, but flexible about how you get there. The destination is fixed; the route is negotiable.

REFLECTION QUESTIONS

1. What "one way" have you been convinced was the only path to your destiny?
2. When has a closed door in your past actually led to something better?
3. Where are you currently crying at a closed door instead of looking for open ones?
4. What person have you elevated to "idol" status, believing your success depends entirely on them?

ACTION STEPS

1. Map alternative routes: For your main goal, brainstorm at least ten completely different ways to achieve it.
2. Reduce dependence: If you're overly dependent on one person, opportunity, or path, deliberately create backup options this week.
3. Study the redirected: Research three successful people whose original path was blocked and who succeeded through an entirely different route.
4. Trust the timing: Write down three past "disappointments" that actually redirected you toward something better. Let this build faith for current closed doors.

10. NOT EVERYONE WILL GO WITH YOU

You began your journey with some people who will not get to the finish line with you. Not everyone who begins with you will finish with you. Not everyone will go with you on this journey.

Some people will start with you and later veer off to go on their own journey. They have their own lives to live, their own dreams to pursue. They weren't born on this earth to help you fulfill your own dream.

THE ENTITLEMENT TRAP

People have a sense of entitlement and expect that people who have been friends with them for years owe them allegiance and should stay with them no matter what else is happening in their own lives. People don't owe you allegiance or everlasting

loyalty. People don't owe you forever friendship. Your friendship wasn't cut in a blood covenant.
Nobody vowed to stay with you until the end of time, and even if they did, they can break that commitment because that was delusional—it was a mistake on their part. Nobody knows where life will take them. When life demands that they take a different path from you, should they disobey the call of destiny, betray themselves, and stay with you because they made a covenant of loyalty to you?
Did they come to this world to serve you and your dream, to follow your own path and do nothing for themselves? Nobody owes you such allegiance.

THE NATURAL SELECTION OF RELATIONSHIPS

In fact, there are times when you may have to encourage some friends to pursue their own dream and move in a different direction from you. There are people who were once friends with me who have since walked away from me. I had outgrown some of them. Some of them couldn't stand my philosophy of life. The more I grew, the more my friends fell away from me.
When you grow spiritually, emotionally, and mentally, some people will fall away from you, and you will attract new friends who believe in your philosophy of life. Your job is to make sure you keep growing, keep exploring the possibilities

which present themselves to you. As you do, people who cannot keep up with you will fall away and make room for people who resonate with you on the same frequency to be attracted to you and walk with you.

THE LAW OF RESONANCE

The law of resonance states that we attract things, people, and situations which are on the same frequency and energy level with us.

Think of it like a radio station. As you grow and evolve, your frequency changes. Some people were tuned to your old frequency—they connected with who you were five years ago. But you're not that person anymore. You're broadcasting on a different frequency now. It's not that they're bad people or that you're better than them. You're simply on different wavelengths.

Trying to maintain relationships with people who are no longer on your frequency is exhausting for both parties. They feel like you've changed (which you have). You feel like they don't understand you anymore (which they don't). Both of you might feel abandoned or betrayed, but really, you've just evolved in different directions.

THE MANIPULATION OF GUILT

Some people use emotional manipulation to get their friends to stay with them even when they know that those friends should be pursuing their own dream. People grow. People are attracted to new things. People face challenges which redefine the focus and direction of their lives.

True friendship is not holding on to people tenaciously and refusing to let them go in order to serve your own agenda. That is manipulation. True friendship is allowing people to do what's best for them, what's best for their dream, what's best for their lives and their journey.

THE GIFT OF SOLITUDE

Some people are so insecure. They are scared of going on their journey alone. They feel they need people around them all the time, so they hold on to people whom they should have let go, relationships which no longer serve them, which no longer bring them peace, which no longer bring them value.

You must understand that sometimes you are going to be alone on your journey. Sometimes none of your friends will show up for you. Some battles in life are fought alone. You are forced by life into a position in which you must grow to stand alone if you want to win the battle before you.

Being alone doesn't make you weak. No. In some situations, being alone brings out the best in you, compels you to dig deep into yourself and tap into resources which have lain dormant, which you have not used for a long time because you always had other people to lean on.

When you are forced to lean on yourself and tap into your inner resources, you will be amazed at what you are capable of achieving on your own. You will be amazed at your own strength.

THE SEASONS OF COMPANIONSHIP

Relationships have seasons:

Spring relationships plant seeds—they introduce you to new ideas, new possibilities, new versions of yourself.

Summer relationships provide growth—these are the people who help you flourish, who support your expansion.

Autumn relationships bring harvest—these companions help you reap the rewards of your efforts and celebrate your achievements.

Winter relationships offer rest—these are the people who sit with you in the quiet, the difficult, the dormant seasons.

Some people are meant for one season. Others cycle through multiple seasons with you. Very few—the truly strategic relationships—remain through all seasons across many years.

The mistake is trying to force a spring relationship to function in winter, or clinging to a summer companion when autumn has arrived. Let people fulfill their seasonal purpose without demanding they stay beyond their time.

GRATITUDE WITHOUT BONDAGE

You can be grateful for who people were in your journey without being bound to them forever. You can honor what they contributed without requiring them to contribute indefinitely. You can celebrate the season you shared without demanding they stay for seasons they weren't meant to experience with you.

When someone exits your life, the appropriate response is: "Thank you for what you brought to my journey. I release you to yours."

Not bitterness. Not resentment. Not accusations of betrayal or abandonment. Just gratitude and release.

REFLECTION QUESTIONS

1. Who in your life are you holding onto out of obligation rather than genuine connection?
2. Who might need your permission to pursue their own path without guilt?
3. What relationship are you maintaining out of fear of being alone?
4. When has solitude actually strengthened you more than companionship would have?

ACTION STEPS

1. Conduct a relationship audit: List your close relationships. For each, honestly assess: Are we growing together or growing apart? Does this relationship still serve both of us?
2. Release with gratitude: If there's someone you've been holding onto inappropriately, write them a letter (you don't have to send it) thanking them for their season in your life and releasing them to their own journey.
3. Embrace strategic solitude: Schedule one day this month where you intentionally spend time alone pursuing your goals without social interaction. Notice your strength.
4. Attract your frequency: Define who you're becoming. What values do you hold? What frequency are you broadcasting? Then deliberately create opportunities to meet people on that same frequency.

11. THE NEXT STEP WILL REVEAL ITSELF TO YOU

"When You Are On The Way, The Way Will Reveal Itself To You."
— *Rumi*

Sometimes we get to a crossroad on our journey when we don't know where to turn or the next step to take. We want to make a quick decision because the more we stand there doing nothing, the more life moves on without us. We want to make sure that it is the right choice we are making and not making a mistake that will haunt us in the future.

You may get so desperate to know what to do that

you stay up all night thinking fearful thoughts about your future and wondering if you will continue to grow and advance in your career, business, and assignment.

FEAR DOESN'T BRING CLARITY

Fear doesn't bring you clarity. Fear paralyzes you and keeps you stuck in one position. Fear is the enemy of your progress. In such moments you have to go against the fearful thoughts that plague your mind like an army of dangerous locusts settling down on the green fields of your mind, darkening your consciousness, blocking out the sunlight of clarity, keeping you in a dark and lonely zone.

When you find yourself at such crossroads in life, think through the options and facts, then take a step in the most appropriate direction you think you should go. There is no perfect direction. Every choice has its pros and cons. So instead of being paralyzed by indecision, take a step and move forward.

THE UNFOLDING PATH

When you take a step and move forward, the path will reveal itself to you. The path will unfold itself before you. It will begin to spread out before you like a beautiful tapestry, and you will see exactly how you should navigate the next phase of your journey.

This is one of the most profound spiritual and practical truths about life: the next step only becomes visible when you take the current step.

Think of driving at night with your headlights on. You can only see 200 feet ahead, but as you drive those 200 feet, the next 200 feet become visible. You never see the entire journey, only the stretch immediately before you. But that's enough. You can drive across an entire country with headlights that only illuminate 200 feet at a time.

Life works the same way. You don't need to see the entire path. You just need to see the next step. And that next step will reveal itself when you take the current one.

STOP OVERTHINKING YOUR LIFE

Stop overthinking your life. Stop worrying about things that have not yet happened. Stop worrying about what you're going to do when you get into a particular situation.

Life has a way of showing us what to do, where to go, when the situation presents itself to us. The right action will rise from within you. The right action will rise and come out from a place of knowledge, a place of peace within you. When you need to make that decision, the right action, the next step, will reveal itself to you.

It is good to be proactive, to prepare for eventualities before they happen. It is good to make detailed plans of your life for the things you want to do months ahead or years ahead. However, sometimes you get into situations you didn't plan for, situations that are so complicated that you don't know what to do.

Things do not always work according to plan. Sometimes we face obstacles that we never contemplated or planned for, challenges on our path that were never part of our plan. When these things happen, we are tempted to panic, tempted to start worrying, tempted to give in to anxiety and fear.

TRUST YOUR INNER GUIDANCE

No matter what happens, you should know that there is always an answer to the situations that confront us. There is an answer to the challenges that we face. There's an answer to the obstacles on our path. Do not allow anxiety to take control of your mind.

The next step will reveal itself to you. The solution you need will reveal itself to you. The direction you need to go will reveal itself to you. The answer you need will reveal itself to you. The right door will reveal itself to you. The right relationship will reveal itself to you.

Worry and anxiety will never bring you solutions, will never give you direction, will never bring you clarity. Worry and anxiety just make things worse for you. They bring about restlessness, they shatter your focus, they weaken you, make you lose your hold on the things that matter, things that are important to you in that present situation. Worry and anxiety complicate your life.

Anxiety derails your thinking and sends you on a wasteful, energy-consuming, fruitless activity which produces nothing of value to help you resolve your situation. Worry hinders you from thinking clearly and receiving direction from your intuition. Worry and anxiety keep you awake at night when you ought to be sleeping and resting.

THE POWER OF INTUITION

Your intuition knows things that your conscious mind doesn't know. Your intuition has answers that will take your conscious mind some time to process, and in some cases your conscious mind never comes up with the answers.

Your intuition is not limited by time or space. Your intuition can see things, hear things, perceive things that haven't even happened yet.

You enter a room and immediately your intuition tells you that they have been talking about you, and may even tell you exactly what they were talking about. Your intuition gives you direction in your dream. It shows you situations and events which haven't happened yet and gives you a warning to protect yourself.

An angel appeared to Joseph in his dream and told

him to take Mary and his child Jesus and escape to Egypt because Herod wanted to destroy the child. Joseph obeyed and escaped just before the genocide happened. Joseph followed that direction that came from his intuition, and he saved not only his life but also the life of his wife and child.

Your intuition gives you guidance about your job, business, relationship, career, family, finances, and health. It comes in a way that you will understand. It comes in a way that is familiar to you. It comes in a way that you will receive it.

LEARNING TO LISTEN

The Bible says in Job 33:14-16:
"For God may speak in one way, or in another,
Yet man does not perceive it.
In a dream, in a vision of the night,
When deep sleep falls upon men,
While slumbering on their beds,
Then He opens the ears of men,
And seals their instruction."

"And seals their instruction" means that your intuition finds the very best way to get important, beneficial, and sometimes urgent information across to you.

You should learn to pay attention to your intuition when it is trying to show you what to do, where to go, who to meet, what to say, to get you out of a difficult situation.

Don't be anxious about the next step you will take.

It will come naturally to you. It will reveal itself to you.

THE POWER OF PRAYER

It is in the place of prayer that your desires are sifted by the Holy Spirit, separating the true from the false, the real from the delusions, and the Spiritual from the flesh.

It is in the place of prayer that your heart is drawn into the perfect Will of the Father for your life; deception is exposed; confusion is turned into clarity, fear to faith, cowardice into boldness, darkness to light and weakness into strength.

It is in the place of prayer that the future of your ministry, business, marriage and career is moulded, constructed and birthed; your steps are ordered into purpose; the gifts and talents in you are empowered to find effortless expression; and the warrior in you is unleashed with grace and wisdom to carry out your assignment and fulfil your purpose.

THE KEYS FOR EFFECTIVE PRAYER

1. Have a set time for prayer. Be consistent.
2. Start and end with gratitude.
3. Make a list of what to pray about.
4. Pray for others.

5. Let your heart be open before God.
6. Pour out your heart to God
7. Ask the Holy Spirit to help you.
8. Listen for guidance, direction and definite instructions.
9. Find relevant scripture to use in prayer.
10. Do not rush. You are speaking to your father, not doing grocery shopping.
11. Be consistent in prayer until your desire manifests in your life.
12. Forgive. Release hurt. Let the Lord heal you.
13. Take action on your ideas. Let the Holy Spirit guide you.
14. Receive God's peace in your heart. Let the peace of God dominate in your heart.
15. Learn to sit still in silence and listen

CREATING SPACE FOR GUIDANCE

The next step reveals itself more clearly when you:
Quiet the noise. Turn off the endless input—social media, news, other people's opinions—and create silence.
Trust the timing. The answer will come when you need it, not necessarily when you want it.
Stay in motion. The next step reveals itself to those who are on the move, not to those who are frozen.
Watch for signs. Sometimes God speaks through synchronicities, "coincidences," and patterns.
Journal without judgment. Write whatever comes

to mind without editing. Often, the answer is buried in the stream of consciousness.

THE PRACTICE OF NOT KNOWING

There's a concept called "beginner's mind"—approaching situations without preconceptions, open to all possibilities. This is the mindset that allows the next step to reveal itself.

When you think you already know, you close yourself off to inspiration. When you admit you don't know, you open yourself to guidance.

"I don't know what to do" is not a position of weakness. It's a position of openness. It's the acknowledgment that you need guidance, and that acknowledgment creates space for guidance to come.

Don't fight the not-knowing. Don't panic in the uncertainty. Don't demand immediate clarity. Trust that the next step will reveal itself in perfect timing. For more information on this subject, read my book: Finding Direction.

REFLECTION QUESTIONS

1. What decision are you currently overthinking instead of trusting to reveal itself?

2. When has your intuition guided you correctly in the past?
3. What noise (external or internal) is blocking you from hearing your inner guidance?
4. What would change if you trusted that the next step will reveal itself when you need it?

ACTION STEPS

1. Create silence: Schedule 15 minutes of complete silence (no phone, no input) daily for one week. Notice what arises.
2. Journal your intuition: For 7 days, write down any intuitive hits, hunches, or gut feelings. Track whether they prove accurate.
3. Take the revealed step: If you already sense what your next step is but haven't acted, do it this week.
4. Practice trust: Choose one situation where you're demanding clarity. Consciously choose to trust that the answer will reveal itself in perfect timing.

12. WHEN PERSEVERANCE BECOMES PRISON

They tell you to never give up. Push harder. Try again. Winners never quit. Quitters never win. The victory is just around the corner—one more day, one more attempt, one more sacrifice.

And sometimes, they're right.

But sometimes, they're catastrophically wrong.

THE DARK SIDE OF GRIT

I've watched people destroy themselves in the name of perseverance. I've seen them pour years into dreams that were never meant to be theirs, cling to relationships that had become toxic, chase goals that stopped serving them long ago. They wore their suffering like a badge of honor, their stubbornness like a crown, convinced that giving up would make them weak.

But here's what nobody tells you: sometimes, the strongest thing you can do is walk away.

There's a story about a hiker lost in the wilderness. He has a map, but it's wrong. The trail he's following leads nowhere—deeper into danger, farther from safety. He has two choices: admit he's lost and call for rescue, or keep walking because turning back feels like failure.

Many choose to keep walking. Some of them never make it out.

THE LIE ABOUT GRIT

We've been sold a lie that grit means never stopping, never questioning, never changing course. But real grit isn't blind. Real grit knows the difference between a wall you need to climb and a wall you need to walk around.

The question isn't whether you should give up. The question is: what are you really holding onto, and why?

I believed in my dreams. I wrote my books when people told me I couldn't. I persevered through doubt, through rejection, through criticism. And it worked—those books changed my life, took me to many nations.

But I've also let go of some dreams that weren't working. Projects that consumed me but produced nothing. Relationships that demanded everything and returned emptiness. Paths that once made sense but had become dead ends.

Letting go of those things didn't make me weak. It made me wise.

THE COST OF PERSEVERANCE

You don't want to give up on your dreams before they're realized—that's true. But you also don't want to be seventy years old, still chasing something that was never yours to catch, wondering where your life went.

The trick is knowing the difference.

Every yes to one thing is a no to something else. Every hour you spend on a failing business is an hour you don't spend with your children. Every year you stay in a relationship that's breaking you is a year you're not available for a relationship that could heal you. Every ounce of energy you pour into the wrong dream is energy stolen from the right one.

Perseverance has a cost. Always.

The question you must ask yourself is: what am I sacrificing to stay? And is it worth it?

HOW TO KNOW WHEN ENOUGH IS ENOUGH

Sometimes the answer is yes. The sacrifice is temporary, the goal is worthy, the struggle is shaping you into someone stronger. You're not lost—you're just in the hard part.

But sometimes the answer is no. You're not being refined; you're being destroyed. You're not building something; you're maintaining a ruin. You're not honoring commitment; you're worshiping stubbornness.

Your body knows before your mind does. It shows up as exhaustion that sleep doesn't fix, as anxiety that has no clear source, as a heaviness that follows you everywhere. Your mind is trying to tell you: this is costing too much.

Your joy knows. When you can't remember the last time you felt genuinely excited about the thing you're pursuing, when it's all obligation and no inspiration, when you're pushing yourself forward with guilt instead of passion—your joy is whispering: this isn't yours anymore.

Your relationships know. When the people who love you keep asking if you're okay, when they tell you you've changed, when your pursuit has isolated you or turned you bitter—they're seeing what you can't.

And somewhere deep inside, beneath the noise and the fear of being called a quitter—you know too.

GIVING UP ISN'T THE OPPOSITE OF PERSEVERANCE

Giving up isn't the opposite of perseverance.

Sometimes, it's the highest form of it.

It takes courage to admit you're lost and call for rescue. It takes strength to say, "This isn't working, and I'm brave enough to try something different." It takes wisdom to know that the mountain you're climbing might not be the one you're meant to summit.

I've given up on things. I've walked away from projects, from opportunities, from versions of myself that no longer fit. And every time, on the other side of that letting go, I found something better—not because life rewarded me for quitting, but because I finally had the space and energy to pursue what was actually meant for me.

THE QUESTION OF ENOUGH

Enough effort is when you can look yourself in the mirror and honestly say: "I gave this everything I had to give, and it's still not working."

Enough effort is when you've tried different approaches, asked for help, been flexible and creative, and the door still won't open.

Enough effort is when staying is no longer about the goal—it's about avoiding the fear of being wrong, or the shame of admitting defeat, or the sunk cost of everything you've already invested.

Enough effort is when you realize that the dream was beautiful, but the reality is destroying you.

THE RIGHT TO CHANGE

YOUR MIND

Never doubt yourself—yes, I still believe that. But also: never doubt your right to change your mind.

You are allowed to want something different than you wanted five years ago. You are allowed to discover that the path you're on isn't taking you where you thought it would. You are allowed to honor what you've learned and still choose to walk away.

Giving up on the wrong thing makes room for the right thing.

So ask yourself: Am I persevering because I'm brave, or because I'm afraid? Am I following through because I'm committed, or because I'm trapped? Am I showing grit, or am I just too stubborn to admit I'm lost?

The answers to those questions will tell you everything you need to know.

Sometimes the most courageous thing you can do is keep going. And sometimes, it's finally giving yourself permission to stop.

REFLECTION QUESTIONS

1. What are you persevering in right now? Be honest—is it building you or breaking you?
2. What would you do if you gave yourself permission to stop?
3. What is this pursuit costing you in terms

of health, relationships, joy, and peace?
4. If your best friend were in your exact situation, what would you advise them to do?

ACTION STEPS

1. Do a cost-benefit analysis: Create two columns. List everything this pursuit is giving you vs. everything it's costing you. Be ruthlessly honest.
2. Set evaluation criteria: Write down 3-5 specific signs that would tell you it's time to pivot. If those signs appear, commit to reconsidering.
3. Consult trusted advisors: Talk to 2-3 people who love you and want the best for you. Listen to their observations.
4. Give yourself an expiration date: Choose a specific date (30, 60, or 90 days out) to reevaluate. If clear progress hasn't been made by then, give yourself permission to choose differently.

13. KNOCK ON DOORS

Sometimes we wait too long for things to happen. We wait for opportunities for advancement, success, and financial breakthroughs to come to us. We wait for invitations to attend the right events, enter the right rooms, sit at the right tables, and have conversations with the right people.

But sometimes those opportunities may never find us. Those invitations may never come unless we do something about it.

THE REALITY ABOUT INVITATIONS

The reality about life is that people hardly hand us invitations for free. People hardly hand over the keys to open the really important doors that are before us. The only way to get ourselves into the right rooms with the right people is to find a way to invite ourselves into those places.

You cannot wait endlessly for people to render you some assistance or help. People may not always come through for you. Some people who mean well, who have good intentions, may not come through for you because they are busy handling some emergencies in their own lives.

You must show up for yourself. Wake up and make things happen for yourself.

THE POWER OF INITIATIVE

One of the things you will learn in life is that often good things don't come to us—we have to go to them. We have to find a way to attract them to us. We have to enter the rooms where those good things await us.

Life demands some courageous and bold moves from us before orchestrating situations to align with our deepest desires.

Waiting for something good to happen may be inimical to your progress and detrimental to your success. Waiting may make you miss great opportunities. Stop waiting and start knocking on doors.

It doesn't matter which doors you knock on, good or bad, as long as you knock on doors. You will never know what lies behind those doors until you knock on them and someone opens the door for you from inside the room you wish to enter.

Nothing happens until you knock on doors.

THE VALUE PROPOSITION

Present a value proposition to your target client or customer. Show them the benefits of using your product or service. Show them what they stand to gain by investing in your product, service, expertise, and experience.

Keep knocking on doors. Show people the desired outcomes they stand to benefit from your service and product, show them value and that door will be opened to you.

The key to getting doors opened is not begging. It's presenting irresistible value that makes saying no difficult.

STRATEGIC DOOR-KNOCKING

Not all doors are worth knocking on. Strategic door-knocking means:

Research first. Know who's behind the door before you knock. Don't waste time on doors that lead nowhere.

Prepare your value proposition. Know exactly what you're offering and why it matters to the person you're approaching.

Start with easier doors. Build confidence and refine your approach by knocking on accessible doors first.

Learn from rejections. Every "no" teaches you how to knock better on the next door.

Be persistent without being a pest. Follow up

appropriately, but respect boundaries.
Knock on multiple doors simultaneously. Don't put all your hopes on one door opening.

CREATING YOUR OWN INVITATIONS

Sometimes the best strategy isn't waiting for an invitation or even knocking on existing doors—it's creating your own door.

When traditional publishers rejected my manuscript, I didn't keep knocking on their doors endlessly. I created my own door through self-publishing. That door led to opportunities I never would have found waiting for someone else to let me in.

You can create your own doors by:
- Starting your own business instead of waiting for the perfect job
- Building your own platform instead of waiting for someone to give you one
- Creating your own opportunities instead of waiting for permission
- Becoming the person who opens doors for others instead of just knocking

THE COURAGE TO BE SEEN

Knocking on doors requires visibility. It requires putting yourself out there, risking rejection, facing the possibility of being told no.

Many people never knock because they're afraid of the answer. They convince themselves that not knocking is safer than knocking and being rejected. But not knocking guarantees failure. Knocking at least creates possibility.

The irony is that the more doors you knock on, the less any single rejection matters. When you're only knocking on one door, a "no" feels devastating. When you're knocking on fifty doors, each "no" is just data that brings you closer to a "yes."

THE PROTOCOL FOR DOORS

Remember: doors are opened from the inside. Your job is to knock compellingly enough that someone inside wants to open it. That means:

Know what's on the other side. Research who you're trying to reach.

Make your knock impossible to ignore. Stand out through value, not volume.

Be ready when the door opens. Have your value proposition clear and compelling.

Respect the gatekeepers. They control access. Treat them well.

Follow up appropriately. Persistence, not pestering.

REFLECTION QUESTIONS

1. What doors have you been waiting for someone else to open for you?

2. What stops you from knocking—fear of rejection, lack of preparation, or something else?
3. What value do you bring that would make someone want to open their door to you?
4. What door could you create for yourself instead of waiting for someone else's?

ACTION STEPS

1. Identify 10 doors: Make a list of 10 specific doors (people, companies, opportunities) you could knock on this month.
2. Prepare your knock: Write a 30-second value proposition. What specifically do you offer and why should they care?
3. Knock on one door today: Choose the easiest door on your list and knock today. Send that email, make that call, submit that application.
4. Track your knocks: Keep a journal of every door you knock on, the response, and what you learn. Aim for 20 knocks this month.

14. THE PROTOCOLS FOR OPENING DOORS

Doors do not open by themselves. To force a door open from the outside is criminal and illegal. There is a protocol for opening doors. If you violate this protocol, doors will not be open to you.

This is the protocol: Doors are opened for you by people who are inside where you want to enter.

THE INSIDER ADVANTAGE

Elite social clubs have a standard protocol by which they operate. If you do not observe their protocols, you will not be admitted. Your membership application will be rejected.

Elite social clubs require that someone on the inside should make an introduction for you before your application is considered, accepted and processed.

This is how the world actually works. Doors are opened for you by people who are already inside the room you wish to enter. Doors are opened for you by people who are already doing what you want to do, by people who are successful in the industry, business, profession, ministry you want to enter—people who are pursuing a similar dream to yours.

Trying to force your way into a new industry, community, organization, or network without inside help is futile. There are doors that your money or name will not open for you. No matter how rich you are, you must follow protocol to be accepted.

Someone on the inside must open that door for you.

THE BIBLICAL PROTOCOL

Even Jesus Christ had to go to John the Baptist to get baptised. That was the protocol for becoming a priest and entering ministry. Jesus followed protocol. He didn't force His way into ministry. He submitted to the proper process and protocol.

If Jesus followed protocol, who are you to bypass it?

THE WISDOM INSIDE

There are businesses you want to start, but you cannot be successful without getting the expertise and wisdom from someone on the inside who will guide you and show you how things are done and how to be successful in that business.

Trying to do it on your own is foolish.

If you want to be rich, you need the wisdom of a rich person to open the door for you and show you the way. When Mark Zuckerberg started Facebook, he went to Steve Jobs to get some wisdom on how to operate in that industry. Steve Jobs opened the door and taught him secrets.

The reason why you are struggling and failing financially is because you have zero financial intelligence. You need the door to be opened for you. The reason why your business is failing is because the door has not been opened to you.

You need people to open the door for you.

BUILDING RELATIONSHIPS WITH INSIDERS

Learn to build strong relationships with the right people in the industry, business, enterprise, ministry you want to enter. People are the key to success, the master key to opening doors of success for you.

How to connect with insiders:

Provide value first. Don't approach with your hand out. Approach with something to give.

Be genuinely interested. Learn about them, their journey, their challenges. People help those who care about them.

Show up consistently. Attend events, engage with their content, be present in spaces where they are.
Ask intelligent questions. Show that you're serious, prepared, and worth investing in.
Respect their time. Be clear, concise, and grateful for any access they grant.
Follow through. If they give you advice or an introduction, act on it and report back.

THE LONG GAME

Building relationships with insiders isn't a quick transaction. It's a long-term investment. You may need to spend months or even years demonstrating your value, your character, your seriousness, your integrity before someone opens a significant door for you.
This is why you must start building these relationships now, even before you need them. Plant seeds today that you'll harvest tomorrow.

THE RECIPROCITY PRINCIPLE

Remember: the people who can open doors for you have people who opened doors for them. They understand the system. They know they benefited from insiders helping them, and many of them want to pay it forward.
But they'll only pay it forward to people who remind them of themselves—people who are hungry, humble, prepared, and worthy of the investment.

Show them you're that person.

REFLECTION QUESTIONS

1. Who are the insiders in the field/industry/space you want to enter?
2. What relationships do you need to build that you haven't prioritized?
3. What value could you provide to insiders that would make them notice you?
4. How patient are you willing to be in building these strategic relationships?

ACTION STEPS

1. Identify 5 insiders: List five people who are already where you want to be.
2. Study them: Learn everything you can about their journey, their values, their current projects.
3. Provide value: Find one way to add value to each person (share their content, solve a small problem, make a useful introduction).
4. Make strategic contact: Reach out to one insider this week with a specific, value-forward message (not asking for anything).

END OF PART THREE

You've now learned not just to understand your journey, but to actively pursue it—with courage, despite uncertainty, trusting that the way reveals itself, knowing when to persist and when to pivot, and understanding how to knock on doors and access the rooms where your destiny awaits.

In Part Four, we'll address the internal battles—the comparison, fear, and limiting beliefs that can sabotage your external progress.

15. THE COURAGE TO FIND YOUR WAY

It takes courage to abandon the illusion of one path. It takes strength to admit that the route you've been traveling isn't working and to search for another way. It takes faith to believe that when one door closes, another opens, even when you can't see it yet.

Society will pressure you to stay on the conventional path. Family will question your decisions to deviate. Friends will project their own fears onto your journey. Employers will try to convince you that leaving is a mistake. Partners will make you feel guilty for wanting something different.

But their limitations are not your limitations. Their fears are not your fears. Their one path is not your only path.

THE FRICTION OF MISALIGNMENT

When you're on the wrong path, everything is hard. You have to beg for opportunities. You have to fight for recognition. You have to convince people of your value. You have to push against resistance constantly. You're exhausted, frustrated, unfulfilled. And you think, "This is just how life is. Success requires struggle."

No. What you're experiencing isn't the struggle of growth. It's the friction of being in the wrong place, pursuing the wrong thing, forcing a path that was never yours to walk.

When you're on the right path, things flow. Doors open. Opportunities appear. The right people show up. Your value is recognized naturally. You don't have to beg because what you offer is wanted. You don't have to diminish yourself because the environment values you as you are.

Yes, there will be challenges, but they're the kind that make you stronger, not the kind that break your spirit.

RECOGNIZING YOUR RIGHT PATH

How do you know when you've found one of your thousand ways? Here are the signs:

Energy flows rather than drains. You finish work

tired but fulfilled, not depleted and resentful.

Doors open more than they close. Yes, there are obstacles, but the overall trajectory is forward movement, not constant blockage.

People recognize your value naturally. You don't have to convince them—they recognise it, receive it, and reward it.

Synchronicities increase. The "right person at the right time" moments happen with surprising frequency.

Your intuition says "yes." Beneath any surface fear, there's a deep knowing that this is your path.

Growth happens naturally. You're learning, expanding, evolving without forcing it.

THE COURAGE TO PIVOT

Finding your way often means having the courage to admit: "I was wrong. This isn't it. I need to try something else."

This is not failure. This is wisdom.

Every attempt teaches you something. Every path you try—even if it's not the right one—eliminates one possibility and points you toward others. You're not failing your way through life; you're discovering your way through life.

Thomas Edison didn't fail 10,000 times. He discovered 10,000 ways that didn't work, which brought him closer to the way that did. Your "failed" attempts are data collection. Your "wrong" paths are elimination rounds. Your "mistakes" are education.

The only real failure is refusing to try another way.

THE VOICES OF DOUBT

As you search for your way, you'll encounter voices of doubt—both external and internal.

External doubt: "You're being irresponsible." "You're too old or too young for this." "That'll never work." "Just be grateful for what you have." "You're being selfish." "What makes you think you're special?"

Internal doubt: "What if I'm wrong?" "What if I fail?" "What if I regret this?" "What if I can't do it?" "What if they were right and I was wrong?"

Here's what you need to understand: doubt is not the absence of the right path. Doubt is the companion of every significant change. Courage isn't the absence of doubt—it's action in the presence of doubt.

Every person who found their way felt doubt. Every person who succeeded questioned themselves. Every person who made it to their summit wondered if they were on the wrong mountain.

The difference is they kept walking anyway.

PERMISSION TO EXPLORE

You don't need anyone's permission to find your way, but I'm going to give it to you anyway:

You have permission to try.

You have permission to fail.
You have permission to pivot.
You have permission to disappoint people who want you to stay stuck.
You have permission to choose a path that makes no sense to anyone but you.
You have permission to change your mind.
You have permission to stop doing what's killing you, even if it pays well.
You have permission to pursue what makes you come alive, even if it seems impractical.
You have permission to find your thousand ways.

THE COMMITMENT REQUIRED

Finding your way requires a commitment—not to a specific path, but to the process of discovery.

Commit to movement. Even if you don't know exactly where you're going, commit to not staying stuck.

Commit to learning. Every path teaches you something. Commit to extracting the lessons.

Commit to adaptation. When something isn't working, commit to trying something else rather than forcing it.

Commit to honesty. Be honest with yourself about what's working and what isn't.

Commit to courage. Keep choosing bravery over comfort, growth over safety, possibility over certainty.

YOUR MOUNTAIN, YOUR ROUTE

There is no single correct route to the top of your mountain. There is no one timeline, no one strategy, no one way to build the life you want. Your journey is yours to design. Your path is yours to create. Your summit is yours to define.

Stop looking at other people's maps. Stop comparing your chapter three to someone else's chapter twenty. Stop believing that because their path worked for them, it must work for you. Stop thinking that because the traditional route didn't work out, you're finished.

You're not finished. You're just getting started on finding your actual path.

Let go of the illusion that there's only one way. Embrace the truth that there are a thousand ways. And if those thousand ways don't work, create the thousand and first way.

The mountain is vast. The possibilities are endless. Your potential is limitless.

Stop begging to stay on a path that rejects you. Stop clinging to a route that doesn't fit you. Stop forcing yourself into a journey that wasn't designed for who you are.

Find your way. Walk your path. Climb your mountain.

REFLECTION QUESTIONS

1. What path are you currently on that requires constant convincing, begging, or forcing?
2. When have you experienced the "flow" of being on the right path?
3. Whose permission are you waiting for that you don't actually need?
4. What would you try if you gave yourself permission to explore without guarantees?

ACTION STEPS

1. Honest assessment: Write down where you're experiencing friction versus flow. Be ruthlessly honest.
2. Give yourself permission: Complete this sentence three times: "I give myself permission to..."
3. Try one alternative: This week, explore one completely different approach to your goal.
4. Silence external doubt: For 30 days, stop sharing your explorations with doubters. Protect your courage.

16. A STEP IN THE RIGHT DIRECTION

Your journey begins with a single step. Sometimes your journey may begin with a phone call, a text, an email, a DM, a social media post. Your journey may begin by setting up a meeting, driving to the other side of town for lunch with someone to discuss your ideas and how to materialize them.

There are a thousand ways to your destiny. However, you have to start that journey. You cannot launch yourself into the future while you remain in the past. You cannot take advantage of the opportunities and possibilities around you if you hold on to the success and achievements of the past.

THE PARALYSIS OF PLANNING

Some people have been talking about the same

plan for years but they have never come to a place where they feel it is right for them to support their words with action. They talk a lot but do very little to show their commitment to the actualization of their dream.

Talking about your dream doesn't mean you are serious about it or that you even plan to make it a reality. Some people talk about their dream to impress their friends with their ideas, but they have no intention whatsoever to embark on the journey of actualization to transform that dream into reality.

Such people are cowards. Every time they talk about their dream, they show everyone that they are cowards who have no emotional or mental muscle to pursue the actualization of their dream.

THE PROOF OF DESIRE

It was Mike Murdock who said, "The proof of desire is pursuit."

What this means is that people say many things which they don't really desire, because if they really desired those things they talked about, they would have started pursuing them. But the fact that they have talked about the same thing for years but never took a step in the direction of those things is proof that they don't care about those things. They don't care whether those things become a reality or not.

The proof of desire is that you back up your words

with action. Your empty rhetoric will not change your life or make great things happen for you. The only thing that will make great things happen for you is when you take action on your dream.

THE POWER OF THE FIRST STEP

The first step is the hardest step. It's the step that requires the most courage because it's the step into the unknown. Once you've taken the first step, the second step is easier. The third step is easier still. Momentum builds with each step.

But that first step—that's where most people stop. They stand at the edge of their comfort zone, looking into the unknown, and they freeze. They convince themselves they need more information, more resources, more certainty, more preparation. But here's the truth: you will never feel completely ready. You will never have perfect information. You will never have total certainty. You will never be entirely prepared.

The first step must be taken with imperfect information, incomplete preparation, and inevitable uncertainty. That's what makes it courage.

SMALL STEPS, BIG MOMENTUM

Your first step doesn't have to be dramatic. It doesn't have to be life-changing in itself. It just has to be in the right direction.

If your dream is to start a business: Your first step might be researching similar businesses, or writing a one-page business plan, or talking to one entrepreneur.

If your dream is to write a book: Your first step might be writing 500 words, or outlining three chapters, or researching publishers.

If your dream is to change careers: Your first step might be taking one online course, or attending one networking event, or updating your resume.

If your dream is to move to a new city: Your first step might be visiting that city for a weekend, or researching job markets there, or connecting with someone who lives there.

Small steps. But steps nonetheless. Movement in the right direction.

And here's what happens with small steps: they create momentum. They build confidence. They generate data. They open doors. They attract opportunities. They connect you with people. They transform you from someone who talks about dreams into someone who pursues them.

THE COMPOUND EFFECT OF DAILY ACTION

James Clear, in "Atomic Habits," talks about the power of 1% improvement. If you improve by just 1% every day for a year, you'll be 37 times better at the end of that year. That's the compound effect.

Your destiny isn't built in one massive leap. It's built in daily increments. One step today. Another step tomorrow. Another the day after that.

365 days of small steps will take you further than you can imagine right now. But it starts with today's step.

OVERCOMING ANALYSIS PARALYSIS

Many people get stuck in perpetual planning. They research endlessly. They analyze every variable. They create elaborate strategies. They wait for the perfect moment.

This is analysis paralysis—the illusion of productivity that's actually just sophisticated procrastination.

Planning is important, but planning without action is just daydreaming. At some point, you have to stop planning and start doing. At some point, you have to say, "Good enough. Let's go."

Perfect plans executed never beat imperfect plans executed now.

THE BIAS TOWARD ACTION

Successful people have a bias toward action. When they have an idea, they test it quickly. When they see an opportunity, they move on it fast. When they identify a problem, they address it immediately.

They don't wait for perfect conditions. They create momentum and then refine as they go. They understand that you can't steer a stationary vehicle—you have to be moving to adjust direction.

This doesn't mean being reckless. It means being decisive. It means valuing movement over perfection. It means understanding that imperfect action beats perfect inaction every single time.

YOUR FIRST STEP TODAY

Right now, before you finish this chapter, I want you to take one step. Not tomorrow. Not next week. Not when you're ready.

Today. Right now.

What's one thing you could do in the next hour that would move you toward your dream? It doesn't have to be big. It just has to be real.

- Send one email
- Make one phone call
- Write one page
- Research one option
- Connect with one person
- Apply for one opportunity
- Sign up for one course
- Post one thing
- Create one outline
- Schedule one meeting

One step. Today. Right now.

Because here's the truth: if you can't take a small

step today, you won't take a big step tomorrow. But if you can take a small step today, tomorrow's step becomes possible. And the day after that. And the day after that.

Your destiny isn't waiting for some grand moment. It's waiting for this moment. The moment you decide to stop talking and start walking.

REFLECTION QUESTIONS

1. What have you been talking about for months or years without taking action?
2. What's stopping you from taking the first step? (Be brutally honest—it's probably fear, not lack of resources.)
3. What small step could you take today that would move you in the right direction?
4. What would change in your life if you took one small step every day for the next 90 days?

ACTION STEPS

1. Identify your first step: Write down the smallest possible action you could take toward your goal.
2. Do it within 24 hours: Set a specific time today or tomorrow to take that step. Put it in your calendar.
3. Create a 7-day action plan: List one small

action for each of the next 7 days. Make them specific and achievable.
4. Track your momentum: Keep a journal for 30 days. Write down your daily action, no matter how small. Watch momentum build.

17. YOU MUST PROCEED WITH UNCERTAINTY

Proceeding with uncertainty on your journey is something I never thought was the right way to go. I always thought to be successful you had to be certain, you had to be sure of what you were doing, where you were going, and the outcomes you expected.

But life taught me differently.

Because there are a thousand ways to your destiny, you're never really sure where the path will take you. You never really know what is going to happen on that path.

THE ILLUSION OF CERTAINTY

You choose a path and you follow that path with expectation. There is no hundred percent certainty in anything because situations are fluid.

Things keep changing. You can't have total certainty that everything's going to be alright or "I'm going to have this outcome if I take this position, I will have this outcome with certainty." No, it doesn't happen that way.

There's no certainty. If you're waiting for certainty before you proceed, if you're waiting for certainty before you take action, if you're waiting for certainty before you make a move on your dream, you're going to wait a long time.

Time will pass you by. Opportunities will pass you by. In fact, if you want to be successful, you cannot afford to wait for all the stars to align. You cannot wait for every external thing to be just right. The situation around you will never be perfect enough for you to move.

Waiting for certainty will sabotage you.

THE PARALYSIS OF OVERTHINKING

You are standing at a place where three ways meet and you're about to make a decision and you keep waiting and waiting. Make a choice. Just decide. Just choose what you want and where you want to go and let whatever will happen, happen.

It is fear that makes people hesitate. It is fear that makes people look for certainty before making a move. There is no certainty in this life. You will never know what will happen until you make that move. You will never know the outcomes until you take action.

So, the thing that goes on in your mind and the thing that happens in reality after taking action may be two different things. You are waiting for that perfect situation to be set up for you before you take action, but it never happens. That is not life. That's not reality. Life doesn't happen that way.

GROWTH BEGINS WHERE FAMILIARITY ENDS

Think of it like a seedling breaking through the soil: the moment it leaves the familiar darkness, it faces the uncertainty of sunlight, wind, and rain. Yet, it's precisely in that exposure that it thrives.

Growth begins where familiarity ends. When you cling to the known—the same routines, the same environment, the same excuses—you're not living; you're stagnating. You're choosing the safety of a small, predictable box over the boundless potential of an open horizon.

Progress demands that we shed the weight of the familiar. It asks us to trade the comfort of "good enough" for the thrill of "what could be." Yes, the unknown is daunting. It's filled with questions: What if I fail? What if I'm not ready?

But here's the counterpoint: What if you succeed? What if this leap into uncertainty is the very thing that defines your legacy?

THE PATH REVEALS ITSELF

When you take a step and move forward, the path will reveal itself to you. The path will unfold itself before you. It will begin to spread out before you like a beautiful tapestry, and you will see exactly how you should navigate the next phase of your journey.

This is the mystery and magic of proceeding with uncertainty: the next step only becomes visible when you take the current step. The door only appears when you start walking toward where you think it might be. The way only reveals itself to those who are on the way.

If you wait at the crossroads for perfect visibility, you'll wait forever. But if you choose a direction and start walking, the path illuminates as you go. Always be ready to take the next step you see.

THE ROLE OF INTUITION

When situations present themselves that you didn't plan for, situations that are so complicated that you don't know what to do, the right action will rise from within you. The right action will rise and come out from a place of knowledge, a place of peace within you. When you need to make that decision, the right action, the next step, will reveal itself to you.

Your intuition knows things that your conscious mind doesn't know. Your intuition has answers that will take your conscious mind some time to process, and in some cases your conscious mind never comes up with the answers.

Your intuition is not limited by time or space. Your intuition can see things, hear things, perceive things that haven't even happened yet.

But your intuition can't guide you if you're frozen by the need for certainty. It can only guide you in movement, in action, in proceeding despite not knowing everything.

THE WISDOM OF STRATEGIC UNCERTAINTY

There's a difference between proceeding with uncertainty and proceeding recklessly. Strategic uncertainty means:

You gather the information you can, but you don't wait for perfect information.

You plan as best you're able, but you don't let planning become procrastination.

You assess risks honestly, but you don't let risk assessment become risk avoidance.

You prepare for multiple outcomes, but you don't let contingency planning paralyze you.

You move with eyes open, but you don't demand to see the entire path before taking the first step.

This is wisdom: knowing that some uncertainty is inevitable and proceeding anyway.

THE COST OF WAITING

While you wait for certainty, life is happening. Opportunities are being seized by those who proceeded with uncertainty. Relationships are being formed by those who took the risk. Businesses are being built by those who started before they had all the answers. Books are being written by those who began without knowing if anyone would read them.

The cost of waiting isn't just what you miss—it's who you never become. Every day you wait is a day you don't grow, don't learn, don't develop the muscle of courage that comes only from proceeding despite uncertainty.

TRUSTING THE UNFOLDING

Take a moment to reflect: What's one step you could take today, right now, toward your dream? It doesn't have to be perfect. It doesn't have to be grand. It just has to be a step.

Maybe it's writing the first words of a book, sketching the outline of a business plan, or reaching out to someone who inspires you. The beauty of action is that it creates momentum. One step leads to another, and soon, the fog begins to lift, not because the world has changed, but because you have.

Life is an unpredictable adventure, a journey with no guarantees, no neatly paved roads, and no promises of certainty. Yet, within this unpredictability lies a profound truth: waiting for the perfect moment, the absolute assurance that everything will fall into place, is a trap.

If you wait for certainty before chasing your dreams, you may find yourself standing still while the world moves forward. Success belongs to those who dare to step into the unknown, who embrace uncertainty as a companion rather than a foe.

REFLECTION QUESTIONS

1. What decision are you postponing because you're waiting for more certainty?
2. What's the worst that could realistically happen if you proceeded with uncertainty?
3. What's the cost of continuing to wait for perfect clarity?
4. When have you proceeded with uncertainty in the past and it worked out?

ACTION STEPS

1. Name your uncertainty: Write down specifically what you're uncertain about. Often, naming it reduces its power.
2. Gather enough information: Spend 2 hours (not 2 months) researching. Then decide with what you know.
3. Set a decision deadline: Give yourself a specific date by which you will make

a decision and move, regardless of remaining uncertainty.
4. Proceed with a pilot: Instead of going all-in, take a small test action. Proceed with uncertainty on a small scale to build confidence for larger moves.

18. REBEL AGAINST FEAR ON YOUR JOURNEY TO SUCCESS

Every great journey has its trials, its dragons to slay, its mountains to climb. But often, the most formidable adversary isn't an external force, but an internal one. It's a shadow that whispers doubts, a weight that holds us back, a voice that tells us we're not ready, not capable, not enough.

This unseen enemy, the most significant obstacle on your path to success, is fear.

THE MANY FACES OF FEAR

Fear is not a single, monolithic entity. It is a hydra with many heads, each representing a specific anxiety that can paralyze our minds and prevent us from taking the necessary steps towards our dreams.

Consider the fear of death, a primal terror that can make us cling to the familiar and avoid any risk, even if that risk is essential for growth.

Then there's the pervasive fear of failure, the dread of not measuring up, of falling short of expectations—our own and others'. This fear can prevent us from even starting, trapping us in a cycle of inaction.

The fear of other people's opinions is another potent inhibitor. We worry about judgment, criticism, and ridicule, allowing the potential disapproval of others to dictate our choices and silence our unique voices.

Coupled with this is the fear of rejection, the pain of being turned away, excluded, or deemed unworthy. This fear can make us hesitant to put ourselves out there, to share our ideas, or to connect with others who could support our journey.

The fear of change, even positive change, often brings with it the fear of the unknown. We are creatures of habit, and stepping into unfamiliar territory, leaving behind the comfort of what we know, can be deeply unsettling.

The fear of poverty is a very real and powerful fear, especially in societies where financial security is paramount. The thought of lacking resources, of not being able to provide for oneself or one's loved ones, can drive decisions based on scarcity rather than opportunity.

Similarly, the fear of authority figures can prevent us from challenging the status quo, speaking truth to power, or pursuing unconventional paths that might lead to greater success but require defying established norms.

Public speaking is a common fear, the dread of standing before others and being vulnerable, of stumbling over words or losing one's train of thought. This fear can limit opportunities for leadership and influence.

The fear of going broke is a recurring theme, a constant worry about losing everything, even if one has achieved some level of success. This fear can lead to risk aversion and an inability to invest in further growth.

The fear of abandonment, a deep-seated anxiety about being left alone or losing support, can make us compromise our dreams to maintain relationships, even if those relationships are not serving our highest good.

Perhaps one of the most critical fears for anyone on a journey of success is the fear of taking action on your ideas. We can have brilliant insights and innovative concepts, but if we are too afraid to act on them, they remain just that—ideas, never manifesting into reality.

This inaction is often fueled by the fear of being

mocked, the humiliation of having our efforts or ideas ridiculed by others.

And finally, the fear of public disgrace, the ultimate fear of shame and humiliation on a large scale, can make us play it safe, avoiding any venture that could potentially lead to public failure.

THE PARALYSIS OF FEAR

These fears, in their myriad forms, lead to a state of mental paralysis. They cause us to hesitate when we should act, to doubt our abilities when we should trust our instincts. They cloud our judgment and prevent us from recognizing and utilizing our own unique genius.

This paralysis is the opposite of the momentum required for success. When fear takes hold, the brilliant ideas that once ignited your imagination dim, and the confidence required to pursue them wanes. You become a spectator in your own life, watching opportunities pass by, all because the fear of potential negative outcomes outweighs the desire for positive ones.

THE REBELLION REQUIRED

Success, true and lasting success, demands a radical response to this internal adversary. It demands that you totally rebel against fear. This isn't a passive resistance; it's an active, defiant stance.

It means taking massive action in the direction of your dream, not despite the fear, but often because of it. The very presence of fear often indicates that you are on the cusp of something significant, something that challenges your comfort zone and promises growth.

To shrink from this challenge is to choose stagnation.

It is crucial to understand a fundamental truth: fear is inevitable, but cowardice is a choice.

Fear is a natural human emotion, a primal response designed to protect us from danger. It will always be present when you step into the unknown, when you push your boundaries, when you dare to dream big.

But how you respond to that fear—whether you let it dictate your actions or you choose to move forward despite it—that is where your power lies.

To be a coward is to succumb to fear, to allow it to dictate your destiny. To be brave is to acknowledge the fear and act anyway.

Fear is common; bravery is rare. This rarity is precisely what makes bravery so valuable and so necessary for success.

Be brave. Make the conscious decision to confront your fears, not by eliminating them, but by acting in their presence.

THE DAILY PRACTICE OF COURAGE

The most effective way to rebel against fear is by taking consistent, incremental, daily action on your dream. This isn't about grand, sweeping gestures every now and then. It's about the power of small, deliberate steps taken consistently over time.

Each small action, no matter how seemingly insignificant, builds momentum. It chips away at the edifice of fear, proving to yourself that you are capable, that the imagined dangers are often less formidable than they appear, and that progress is indeed possible.

Think of it as building a muscle. You don't become strong overnight; you do it through regular, disciplined workouts. Similarly, you don't conquer fear in one heroic leap; you do it through consistent, daily acts of courage.

These incremental actions create a positive feedback loop: action leads to small victories, which build confidence, which in turn makes the next action easier. This process transforms the overwhelming mountain of your dream into a series of manageable steps, each one a testament to your bravery.

CHOOSING MOVEMENT OVER PARALYSIS

Your journey to success will inevitably be shadowed by fear. It will manifest in countless forms, attempting to paralyze your mind and stifle your genius.

But remember, fear is a feeling, not a fact. While its presence is inevitable, your response to it is entirely within your control.

Choose bravery over cowardice. Rebel against the mental paralysis by taking consistent, incremental, daily action in the direction of your dreams.

Embrace the discomfort, for it is often a sign that you are on the right path. The world awaits the manifestation of your genius; don't let fear keep it hidden.

Be brave, take action, and watch as your dreams unfold.

REFLECTION QUESTIONS

1. Which specific fear most frequently stops you from taking action?
2. What small action could you take today that would be an act of rebellion against that fear?
3. When have you acted despite fear in the past? What happened?
4. What would your life look like one year from now if you took one small brave action every day?

ACTION STEPS

1. Name your fears: Write down the top

5 fears that paralyze you. Naming them reduces their power.
2. Daily courage practice: For the next 30 days, do one thing each day that scares you (something appropriate and safe, but outside your comfort zone).
3. Track courage moments: Keep a journal of every time you act despite fear. Notice how your capacity for courage grows.
4. Find courage models: Identify three people who inspire you with their courage. Study how they handle fear.

19. OVERCOMING THE FEAR OF POVERTY

The fear of poverty is a silent, insidious shadow that can creep into the corners of our minds, paralyzing ambition and stifling dreams. It is a primal anxiety, deeply rooted in our survival instincts, whispering tales of hardship, deprivation, and loss.

This fear is not merely about the absence of money; it is a profound apprehension of what that absence might entail: the inability to provide for loved ones, the erosion of dignity, the loss of security, and the crushing weight of societal judgment.

Yet, within this very fear lies a powerful catalyst for growth, a hidden opportunity to redefine our relationship with abundance and resilience.

THE ORIGINS OF SCARCITY THINKING

To truly overcome the fear of poverty, we must first understand its origins. For many, it stems from personal experiences of scarcity, witnessing financial struggles in childhood, or living through periods of economic uncertainty. These experiences etch themselves into our subconscious, creating a blueprint of anxiety that can resurface even when our circumstances improve.

For others, fear is a product of societal narratives—the constant bombardment of messages equating wealth with worth, success with solvency, and poverty with failure. The media often paints a stark picture of financial struggle, reinforcing the idea that a lack of material possessions is synonymous with a lack of value.

This external pressure can be just as potent as internal memories, shaping our deepest anxieties about financial stability.

Moreover, the fear of poverty is often intertwined with a fear of the unknown. The future is inherently uncertain, and financial stability can feel like a fragile construct, easily shattered by unforeseen events: a sudden job loss, an unexpected illness, or a global economic downturn.

HOW FEAR MANIFESTS

The pervasive nature of this fear can manifest in various detrimental ways:

Obsessive saving at the expense of joy. An unhealthy focus on saving every penny, even at the cost of necessary self-care or experiences that bring fulfillment.

Scarcity mindset. Viewing opportunities through a lens of limitation rather than potential, preventing calculated risks or investments in oneself.

Chronic stress and anxiety. Constant worry about money breeding stress, anxiety, and even depression.

Relationship strain. Financial worry leading to arguments, resentment, and isolation in relationships.

Shame and inadequacy. Deep sense of shame causing withdrawal from social interactions or hiding perceived financial shortcomings.

The fear of poverty can rob us of our present peace and future possibilities, trapping us in a cycle of worry that is often more debilitating than any actual financial hardship.

SHIFTING YOUR RELATIONSHIP WITH MONEY

Overcoming the fear of poverty is not

about ignoring financial realities; it is about transforming our relationship with them. It begins with a conscious shift in perspective, recognizing that true wealth extends far beyond monetary value.

It encompasses our health, our relationships, our knowledge, our skills, and our inner resilience. When we broaden our definition of wealth, the fear of losing money becomes less absolute, less terrifying.

One powerful step is to cultivate a mindset of abundance. This doesn't mean blindly ignoring challenges, but rather focusing on what we have, rather than what we lack.

Practicing gratitude for current blessings, no matter how small, can rewire our brains to see opportunities and resources where we once saw only scarcity. It's about understanding that creativity, resourcefulness, and determination are far more valuable assets than any bank balance, for these are the tools that can rebuild and create anew, regardless of external circumstances.

PRACTICAL STEPS

While mindset is crucial, practical steps are equally important in mitigating the fear of poverty:

Financial literacy: Educating ourselves about budgeting, saving, investing, and debt management can demystify money and empower

us to make informed decisions.
Emergency fund: Creating a realistic budget and building an emergency fund provides a tangible sense of control and security.
Multiple income streams: Developing diverse skills and streams of income acts as a buffer against economic shocks.
Continuous learning: Investing in personal and professional development increases earning potential and builds self-reliance.
Strong networks: Building professional relationships and exploring new opportunities opens doors that fear might otherwise keep shut.

THE COST OF FEAR-BASED LIVING

While you protect yourself from potential poverty, consider what you're sacrificing:
Opportunity cost: Every safe choice is a potentially transformative opportunity not taken.
Health cost: Chronic financial anxiety takes a real toll on physical and mental health.
Relationship cost: Financial fear can make you transactional, suspicious, or controlling in relationships.
Joy cost: You miss present moments because you're always worrying about future scarcity.
Growth cost: You don't invest in yourself, your education, or your development because you're hoarding resources.

REDEFINING SECURITY

True financial security isn't a number in a bank account. It's:
Skills that are valuable in any economy
A network of relationships built on mutual support
Confidence in your ability to create value
Resilience to adapt when circumstances change
Peace that comes from knowing your worth isn't tied to your net worth
You can lose money and still have security if you have these things. You can have money and lack security if you don't.

MOVING FORWARD

Ultimately, overcoming the fear of poverty is an ongoing journey of self-discovery and resilience. It involves acknowledging the fear, understanding its roots, and then actively choosing to cultivate a different narrative.

It's about recognizing that setbacks are not failures, but opportunities for learning and growth. It's about understanding that our worth is not tied to our net worth, and that true success is measured not by the size of our bank account, but by the richness of our lives, the depth of our connections, and the impact we have on the world. Let us not allow the shadow of scarcity to dictate our lives. Instead, let us embrace the light of possibility, armed with knowledge, resilience, and an unwavering belief in our own capacity to thrive, regardless of the economic tides.

REFLECTION QUESTIONS

1. What specific financial situation triggers your deepest fear?
2. Where did your fear of poverty originate —personal experience, family patterns, or societal messages?
3. How has fear of poverty actually limited your opportunities or growth?
4. What would you do differently if you believed in your ability to create value regardless of circumstances?

ACTION STEPS

1. Calculate your "enough" number: What would provide genuine security without excess? Write it down. Work toward that, not infinite accumulation.
2. Invest in earning ability: This month, invest in one skill, course, or relationship that increases your ability to create value.
3. Build one additional income stream: Start exploring one way to diversify your income, even if small.
4. Practice resourcefulness: Once this week, solve a problem with creativity rather

than money. Build confidence in your resourcefulness.

20. DON'T SET YOURSELF ON FIRE TO KEEP OTHERS WARM

Some people want to act nice to make other people happy. They will make themselves uncomfortable to make other people happy. They will deny themselves, they will put themselves through pain to make other people like them.

This is foolishness.

THE QUESTION OF BOUNDARIES

How far would you go to be liked and accepted by other people? How far will you go to seek the approval and validation of other people? What will you do to gain the recognition of people around

you?
Don't set yourself on fire to keep others warm.
Don't deprive yourself of happiness because you think by doing so people will see you as a kind person. You want to be seen as altruistic, a Mother Teresa who gives up all personal comfort so that others may enjoy some of the basic necessities of life.

When you have financial and material resources, some people expect you to provide for them, as if it is your duty and responsibility to solve their problems. The relatives of the rich pester them for money and ask them to solve their financial problems as if they are responsible for creating those problems.

And if the rich do not help them, they are seen as unkind and wicked. The sad thing is that even if you help some of these people, they will be ungrateful for what you did for them.

THE TRAP OF MARTYRDOM

Don't go broke in order to provide for other people. Don't go broke to rescue people from poverty. Don't go naked and give other people your clothes in order to keep them warm.

If you set yourself on fire to keep other people warm, you are foolish. You will ruin yourself to make other people happy.

The martyr complex is seductive. It feels noble. It looks selfless. Society celebrates it. But it's ultimately destructive—to you and to the people you're "helping."

When you sacrifice your wellbeing for others, you:
- Model unhealthy boundaries
- Enable dependency rather than empowerment
- Build resentment that poisons relationships
- Deplete yourself until you have nothing left to give
- Teach people that your needs don't matter

HELP WITHOUT HARM

There's a difference between generosity and self-destruction:

Generosity: Giving from overflow without depleting yourself.

Self-destruction: Giving from deficit, harming yourself to help others.

Generosity: Empowering others to solve their problems.

Self-destruction: Solving others' problems for them, creating dependency.

Generosity: Maintaining boundaries while offering support.

Self-destruction: Eliminating boundaries to accommodate others.

Generosity: Helping those who help themselves.

Self-destruction: Enabling those who refuse to help themselves.

You can be kind without being a martyr. You can

be generous without being depleted. You can help others without harming yourself.

THE ILLUSION OF INDISPENSABILITY

You should understand that no man, no woman, no job, no business, no country, no environment, no relationship, no opportunity, no organisation, no situation, determines your destiny and outcomes in life.

Do not be scared of people, situations, organisations, environments, because you think without something or someone you will fail. It's a lie.

There are a thousand ways to your destiny. When one door closes, another door will open to you.

Life does not revolve around you. It is in human nature to overestimate our importance and value in people's lives and in what we do. We think: "Without me this business will fail," "Without me my spouse will suffer, where will he find a woman like me who will give him all I give him?"

This is delusional.

No business depends on you. Without you the business will do much better, and even if it fails, someone else will come up with a better idea, product, or service to meet that need. When Steve Jobs died, Apple did much better. The business was not dependent on him.

No relationship revolves around you. Without you

your partner will have a better, happier, and more peaceful life.

HEALTHY BOUNDARIES ARE LOVE

Setting boundaries isn't selfish; it's sustainable. It's the only way to give genuinely without building resentment. It's the only way to help without enabling.

Boundaries protect:
- Your energy for what matters most
- Your resources for strategic deployment
- Your peace from unnecessary drama
- Your relationships from resentment
- Your ability to give long-term

Without boundaries, your generosity has an expiration date. You'll burn out, shut down, and have nothing left to give anyone—including yourself.

STAY HUMBLE

Some of you lie to yourselves and think that "you control the marriage and your spouse is at your mercy." What nonsense. Nothing revolves around you. Stay humble or you will be humiliated.

There were friends who thought I would suffer without them. They tried to punish me by taking away their friendship. But there's no vacuum in life. When one door closes, other doors open.

When they left, God opened doors, gave me friends who brought greater value and benefits.

Humble yourself. Life does not revolve around your small head. A thousand people who are better than you are waiting on the sidelines to replace you in that business and in that relationship if anything happens to you or if you walk away.

REFLECTION QUESTIONS

1. Where are you currently setting yourself on fire to keep others warm?
2. What are you afraid will happen if you establish healthier boundaries?
3. Who in your life consistently takes without reciprocating?
4. What resentments are you building by giving beyond your capacity?

ACTION STEPS

1. Identify your martyrdom: Write down three ways you're sacrificing your wellbeing for others.
2. Set one boundary: This week, say "no" to one request that would deplete you.
3. Give from overflow only: For 30 days, only give what you can give without resentment or depletion.
4. Evaluate relationships: List your relationships. Mark which ones are

reciprocal and which are one-sided. Adjust your investment accordingly.

END OF PART FOUR

You've now mastered the internal battles that sabotage external success: comparison that steals joy, inauthenticity that attracts the wrong people, oversharing that depletes power, fear that paralyzes action, poverty thinking that limits possibility, and boundary-lessness that leads to burnout.

In Part Five, we'll explore practical wisdom for accelerating your journey—from creating luck to following mentors to building visibility to making strategic choices about what to pursue and what to release.

---

21. COMPARISON IS DOING VIOLENCE TO YOUR OWN SOUL

"Comparison is the thief of joy."
— Theodore Roosevelt

There's always a tendency to compare yourself to other people. There's a tendency to compare yourself to people who are better than you, people who you think are better than you, people who you think are on the same level with you. There's a tendency to look at people, what they're doing with their lives, and look at your own life to see if you measure up to whatever is going on in their lives.

Comparing yourself to people—whether you think you're better than them or they're better than you—is always a mistake.

WHY COMPARISON IS VIOLENT

Your journey is different from their journey. Your destination is different from their destination. Your dream is different from their dream. You are not the same with these people you compare yourself with.

It doesn't matter if you attended the same schools, colleges, and universities. It doesn't matter if you were colleagues in the same company. You and those people have different lives.

This is why there should be no basis for comparison. You don't have the same abilities, the same personalities, the same world views, the same opportunities, the same pedigree, the same advantages.

Comparing yourself with people who have had a completely different life trajectory than you is unwise. There are people who have had solid foundations laid for them by their parents and now they are doing well financially, but your parents never did any such thing for you. Everything you have, you made happen by your discipline, consistency, struggle, and hard work. Nobody laid a financial foundation for you, but you keep comparing yourself to other people.

THE DARK CLOUD OF COMPARISON

Comparison is negative energy which causes a dark cloud to come over your mind and your thinking. Instead of having gratitude for the good things you have in your life, you start feeling bad and bitter about what you don't have, what you've not accomplished.

Comparison is negative energy which drains you emotionally and slows you down. Comparison makes you ignore your wins and start looking at your disadvantages and your losses. Comparison puts you in a competitive mode, in which you compete with everyone around you instead of collaborating with them.

You think you have something to prove. Bu you have nothing to prove to anyone. You don't have to show them how successful and accomplished you are. You owe nobody an explanation for your life. You don't have to explain yourself or explain your life to anyone.

THE SOCIAL MEDIA TRAP

Social media has weaponized comparison. You're scrolling through curated highlight reels of other people's lives while sitting in your regular, messy, unfiltered reality. Of course you feel inadequate.

But remember: you're comparing your behind-the-scenes to everyone else's highlight reel. You're comparing your chapter 3 to their chapter 20. You're comparing your rough draft to their published version.

It's not a fair comparison. It was never meant to be a comparison.

Researchers discovered that over 65% of people who use Facebook are depressed after using that social media app. The reason? Constant comparison with carefully curated versions of other people's lives.

YOUR UNIQUE RACE

Stop comparing yourself to other people. Measure yourself by the standards you've set for yourself, by the goals you've set for yourself. Measure yourself by the demands you've placed on yourself. Live your life by your own rules. Run your own race at your own pace. Live your life on your own terms.

There is no universal timeline for success:
- Some people bloom at 20, others at 60
- Some people take the fast track, others take the scenic route
- Some people sprint, others marathon
- Some people climb one mountain, others scale many smaller hills

None of these is better or worse. They're just different. And different doesn't require comparison.

THE ONLY COMPARISON THAT MATTERS

If you must compare, compare yourself to your past self:
- Am I better than I was last year?
- Have I grown in the areas I wanted to grow?
- Am I closer to my goals than I was six months ago?
- Am I living more aligned with my values than I was yesterday?

This is the only comparison that serves you. This is the only comparison that generates motivation rather than discouragement. This is the only comparison that honors your unique journey.

CELEBRATING OTHERS WITHOUT DIMINISHING YOURSELF

You can admire someone's success without making it mean you're failing. You can be inspired by someone's journey without feeling condemned by your own. You can celebrate someone's wins without comparing them to your losses.

Their success doesn't diminish your potential. Their timeline doesn't invalidate yours. Their path doesn't make yours wrong.

There's enough success, enough opportunity,

enough abundance for everyone. Someone else winning doesn't mean you're losing. Someone else being blessed doesn't mean you're cursed. Someone else arriving doesn't mean you're behind.

THE PRACTICE OF GRATITUDE

The antidote to comparison is gratitude.

When you're genuinely grateful for what you have, you can't simultaneously resent what you don't have. When you're focused on your blessings, you're not focused on someone else's advantages. When you're celebrating your progress, you're not lamenting someone else's faster progress.

Gratitude shifts your focus from what's missing to what's present. From what they have to what you have. From where you're not to where you are.

This isn't toxic positivity or denial of real challenges. This is choosing to honor your journey without invalidating it through constant comparison to someone else's.

REFLECTION QUESTIONS

1. Who do you most frequently compare yourself to, and why?
2. How does comparison specifically affect your mood, energy, and motivation?
3. What progress have you made that you're ignoring because you're focused on someone else's progress?

4. If you stopped comparing yourself to others, what would you focus on instead?

ACTION STEPS

1. Social media detox: Take a 7-day break from the platforms where you compare yourself most. Notice the difference.
2. Track your progress: Create a "wins journal." Every day, write down three things you accomplished or improved, comparing only to your past self.
3. Celebrate others authentically: When you notice comparison arising, deliberately celebrate that person's success without making it mean anything about you.
4. Define your own metrics: Write down the 5 metrics by which you will measure your own success, independent of anyone else's journey.

22. BE AUTHENTIC

Don't try to change yourself to be accepted by or to please everyone. Become more of who you are. When you do, you will attract people who are searching for you—people who will love you for who you are, people who will accept your uniqueness and self-expression.

THE MAGNETIC POWER OF AUTHENTICITY

There are people who have been searching for someone exactly like you. Someone with your ideas. Someone who sees the world the way you do. When you remain true to yourself, when you function from a place of authenticity, they will be attracted to you like a moth to a flame.

I have posts on Instagram and Facebook attracting hundreds of comments from people thanking me for being me. Many of them say if they had seen my post sooner, they would have made better life choices.

There are people who will feed on your authenticity, and nothing else will satisfy them.

THE COST OF PERFORMANCE

When you perform instead of being authentic, you pay a steep price:

You attract the wrong people. People who like your performance, not the real you. When you eventually get tired of performing (and you will), they'll leave—confused about why you "changed" when really, you just stopped pretending.

You exhaust yourself. Maintaining a performance requires constant energy. You're always monitoring, adjusting, censoring, performing. It's exhausting.

You lose yourself. The more you perform, the less you remember who you actually are. The mask becomes so familiar that removing it feels strange.

You create shallow connections. People connect with your performance, not with you. The relationships feel hollow because they are—they're based on fiction.

You resent your success. Even if the performance works and you get the approval you sought, it feels empty because you know they don't actually see you.

THE FEAR OF REJECTION

The reason people perform instead of showing up authentically is simple: fear of rejection.

"If they see the real me, they won't accept me. If I show my true self, they'll judge me. If I'm fully honest, they'll leave."

But here's the paradox: when you're inauthentic to avoid rejection, you're already rejecting yourself. You're saying, "The real me isn't good enough, so I'll hide it."

That's the deepest rejection of all—self-rejection.

And the cruel irony? Even when you win approval through performance, it doesn't feel like acceptance because you know they're not accepting the real you. They're accepting your performance.

You can never win by being inauthentic. Either they reject your performance (and you feel rejected), or they accept your performance (and you still feel unseen).

The only way to win is authenticity.

THE LIBERATION OF "NOT FOR EVERYONE"

Here's a truth that will set you free: You are not for everyone, and that's not a problem.

Your authentic self will repel some people. And that's perfect. Those people weren't your people anyway. By repelling them quickly through authenticity, you save everyone time.

Meanwhile, your authentic self will deeply

resonate with other people—your actual people. These connections will be real, deep, nourishing, and sustainable because they're based on truth, not performance.

Don't try to be for everyone. Be completely, unapologetically for your people. They're searching for you. Make yourself easy to find by being undeniably, recognizably you.

AUTHENTIC DOESN'T MEAN UNFILTERED

Being authentic doesn't mean sharing everything, having no boundaries, or being recklessly transparent.

Authenticity means being true to your values, expressing yourself genuinely within appropriate contexts, and not pretending to be someone you're not to gain approval.

You can be authentic and still have privacy. You can be authentic and still have discretion. You can be authentic and still have boundaries.

Authenticity is about alignment between your internal truth and external expression—not about oversharing or lacking discernment.

BUILDING CONFIDENCE IN AUTHENTICITY

If you've been performing for a long time, showing up authentically can feel terrifying. Here's how to build that confidence:

Start small. Share one authentic thought in a safe space. Notice that you survive.

Find your people first. Seek out communities where authenticity is valued. Practice there before going public.

Document your values. Write down what you truly believe, value, and stand for. This becomes your authenticity anchor.

Accept the discomfort. The first times you show up authentically will feel vulnerable. That's growth, not danger.

Celebrate alignment. Notice how much better it feels when you're aligned—even if fewer people approve.

THE UNEXPECTED REWARDS

When you commit to authenticity, surprising things happen:

Your energy increases. You're no longer draining yourself with performance. You have more energy for creation.

Your confidence grows. Standing in your truth, regardless of response, builds unshakeable self-respect.

Your work improves. Authentic expression is always more powerful than performed expression.

Your relationships deepen. The connections you make are real and reciprocal.

Your success feels meaningful. When you succeed

as yourself, the victory is actually yours.
Don't conform. Be authentic.

REFLECTION QUESTIONS

1. In what areas of your life are you performing rather than being authentic?
2. What are you afraid will happen if you show up as your real self?
3. Who in your life knows and accepts the real you? What do those relationships feel like?
4. What would change if you gave yourself permission to be fully authentic?

ACTION STEPS

1. Identify your performance: Write down three ways you're currently performing or conforming instead of being authentic.
2. Define your authentic self: Write down 10 true things about yourself—values, beliefs, perspectives, preferences—that you sometimes hide.
3. Take one authentic action: This week, express one authentic truth you've been hiding (in an appropriate context).
4. Find your people: Join one community, group, or space where authenticity and individuality are celebrated. Start showing up as yourself there.

23. NOBODY NEEDS TO KNOW

There are things which ought to be private. There are things which no one needs to know. There are wins and achievements that you should keep to yourself. There are wins that even members of your family should not know about. There are wins that you should not tell your friends.

Nobody needs to know about your new house.

Nobody needs to know about your latest asset acquisition.

Nobody needs to know about your plans and your next big move.

Nobody needs to know about the new opportunity which presented itself to you.

Nobody needs to know about the favour you just experienced.

Nobody needs to know about what is going on in your relationship or in your marriage.

Nobody needs to know what is going on in your

home.
Privacy is power. What people don't know they cannot destroy.

THE OVERSHARING EPIDEMIC

Some people feel the need to tell everyone everything in an attempt to win their validation and approval. They tell people things which they ought to keep private. They reveal things which they ought to keep secret. They don't understand that the information they give people becomes ammunition and a weapon in the hands of their enemies to attack and sabotage them.

Why do you feel pressured to let people know what is going on in your life? Why do you feel it necessary to share intimate details of your life with complete strangers on social media? Why do you feel the need to let people know how much you earn, how many assets you have, what your next big move is?

Why do you share things which you ought to keep to yourself?

THE ROOT: LOW SELF-ESTEEM

It is because of low self-esteem. It is because you derive your worth and value from the approval and validation of people who mean nothing to you.

It is strange how the likes and comments of total strangers on people's posts on social media affect and determine how people feel about themselves. You make a post on Facebook. Total strangers say horrible things about you on that post. This makes you feel bad about yourself, hate yourself, and you become depressed.

How can the opinions of total strangers affect you so much that you allow it to define who and what you are and you become depressed? Why do you allow the opinions of people who don't know anything about you determine how you feel about yourself, feel about your life?

The opinions of people should have zero effect on how you feel about yourself.

THE DANGER OF EXPOSURE

In an attempt to be liked, accepted, and approved, people share things which they ought to keep private. The more likes they garner from their posts, the more they feel it necessary to share more of their private lives.

But this creates danger:

Your wins become targets. People who envy you will work to undermine what you've achieved.

Your plans can be sabotaged. When you announce plans prematurely, people can block, copy, or interfere with them.

Your joy gets polluted. Sharing your happiness with people who don't genuinely celebrate you contaminates it with their negativity.

Your relationships suffer. Broadcasting intimate

details creates voyeurism and invites unwanted opinions into private matters.

Your energy gets drained. You're constantly performing for an audience instead of living your life.

STRATEGIC SILENCE

Privacy isn't secrecy. Privacy is wisdom. It's knowing that:

Not everything needs an audience. Some moments are sacred, meant only for you or your closest circle.

Timing matters. Share your wins after they're secured, not while they're forming.

Discretion protects. What people don't know, they can't attack, copy, or sabotage.

Mystery is magnetic. People respect what they can't fully access.

Your energy is precious. Don't waste it on validation from people who don't matter.

WHAT TO PROTECT

Your next moves: Don't announce your plans. Let your results be the announcement.

Your finances: How much you earn, what you own, what you're building financially—keep it private.

Your relationships: The intimate details of your marriage, dating life, family dynamics—not for public consumption.

Your strategy: How you're building, what you're

learning, who you're working with—protect your competitive advantage.

Your wins: Celebrate privately or with your inner circle first. Let others discover your success through your results, not your announcements.

Your struggles: You don't owe anyone a real-time broadcast of your challenges. Process them privately or with trusted advisors.

THE EXCEPTION: STRATEGIC SHARING

There are times when sharing is strategic:

When teaching: Sharing your journey to help others learn from your experience.

When building: Sharing your work to attract collaborators, clients, or opportunities.

When inspiring: Sharing your story to encourage others who are on similar paths.

But even then, share the lesson, not the intimate details. Share the principle, not the private information. Share the outcome, not the process.

BUILDING INTERNAL VALIDATION

If your sense of value and worth is tied to the validation of people on social media, then you will reveal things you ought to keep private. You will place your happiness in the hands of random people on social media. This is foolish.

If your happiness is dependent on the positive feedback you receive from people, then those same people have the power to make you feel bad about yourself by giving you negative feedback. Nobody should have such power over you emotionally.

Build your validation internally. Derive your worth from your own assessment of your character, your effort, your growth—not from the approval of strangers.

Privacy is power. Guard it.

REFLECTION QUESTIONS

1. What have you been oversharing that you should keep private?
2. Why do you feel compelled to share things publicly—validation, approval, or something else?
3. What has oversharing cost you in terms of energy, peace, or actual outcomes?
4. Where do you currently derive your sense of worth—from within or from external validation?

ACTION STEPS

1. Audit your sharing: Review your social media posts from the past month. Identify what you shared that would have been better kept private.
2. 30-day privacy experiment: For the next

30 days, share only strategic content. Keep wins, plans, and personal matters private. Notice the difference.
3. Build internal validation: Daily practice: Write down three things you did well today that no one else knows about. Celebrate them privately.
4. Create a privacy filter: Before sharing anything, ask: "Does anyone need to know this? What do I gain by sharing? What could I lose?"

PART FIVE: Practical Wisdom For The Journey.

24. THE TRUTH ABOUT LUCK

We've all heard the stories. The overnight success who "got lucky." The lottery winner whose life changed in an instant. The entrepreneur who was in the right place at the right time.

It's tempting to look at these people and chalk their success up to luck. But here's the truth most people don't talk about: luck isn't something that just happens to you. It's something you create.

LUCK IS PREPARATION MEETING OPPORTUNITY

Luck isn't the universe's random gift. It's a byproduct of preparation, persistence, and a mindset that's ready to seize opportunities when they arise.

While it may seem like some people are just

born under a lucky star, the reality is that they've positioned themselves for success through consistent effort and by embracing a mentality of abundance.

One of the biggest myths about luck is that it happens in a vacuum. But when you look closer at those so-called "lucky" moments, you'll often find years of hard work, dedication, and preparation.

Take any successful person—an athlete, an artist, a business leader. Sure, they may have had a big break, but if they weren't prepared to seize the moment, that opportunity would've passed them by. They created their luck by consistently showing up and honing their skills, even when no one was watching.

Start building your skills today. Whether it's in your career, a passion project, or personal growth, preparation is the foundation for future opportunities. The more you invest in yourself, the more ready you'll be when your moment comes.

THE MINDSET OF THE LUCKY

There's a saying that "you get what you expect." This is particularly true when it comes to luck.

People who believe they're lucky tend to notice more opportunities, take more risks, and see setbacks as temporary rather than permanent. Their mindset is wired for abundance, and because of that, they're more likely to create and attract success.

On the other hand, if you believe that good things never happen to you, you'll subconsciously block opportunities. You'll be so focused on what's going wrong that you'll miss the doors opening right in front of you.

Shifting your mindset from scarcity to abundance is the first step toward creating your own luck.

Adopt a mindset of possibility. Start expecting good things to happen in your life, and actively look for opportunities in every situation. The more you focus on abundance, the more it will flow into your life.

LUCK FAVORS THE PERSISTENT

Luck often comes disguised as hard work. Many people give up when success doesn't happen right away. They think that if something doesn't work out immediately, it's a sign that it wasn't meant to be.

But the truth is, most successful people faced numerous failures and setbacks before they "got lucky." The difference is they didn't quit. They kept pushing, refining their approach, and learning from their mistakes.

Think of luck like planting seeds. You may not see immediate results, but if you keep tending to your garden, eventually, something will grow. The more seeds you plant—through effort, resilience, and a willingness to try new things—the more chances you give yourself to get "lucky."

Keep going, even when the results aren't immediate. Stay persistent in your efforts, and understand that every setback is setting you up for future success. Remember, the only way to fail is to stop trying.

SERENDIPITY REQUIRES OPENNESS

Opportunities don't always come wrapped in the package you expect. Sometimes, what feels like a detour is actually the right path. Being open to serendipity means recognizing that luck can show up in unexpected ways.

It could be a chance encounter, an unforeseen challenge, or even a failure that leads you to something better. The key is to stay flexible and open-minded.

Many people miss out on opportunities because they're so focused on one specific outcome. But luck often requires us to pivot, adapt, and embrace the unknown. By being open to different possibilities, you allow room for luck to find you.

Let go of rigid expectations and embrace the idea that the path to success may look different than you planned. Stay curious, adaptable, and open to new possibilities.

THE POWER OF PROXIMITY

You become more "lucky" when you position

yourself in environments where opportunities exist. This means:

Being where the action is. If you want to be a filmmaker, you need to be in spaces where filmmakers gather. If you want to build a tech startup, you need to be in tech communities.

Surrounding yourself with ambitious people. The people around you either lift you up or pull you down. Positive, driven individuals expose you to new opportunities and encourage you to grow.

Showing up consistently. Luck favors those who are present. Attend events. Engage in communities. Be visible. The more you show up, the more chances you have for "lucky" encounters.

THE BIAS TOWARD ACTION

Luck favors those who take action. You can't wait for the perfect moment, the right conditions, or for luck to fall into your lap. It's about taking small, consistent steps every day toward your goals.

Action creates momentum, and momentum creates opportunities. The more proactive you are, the more likely you are to encounter those moments that others might call luck.

Luck is often the result of simply showing up. It's about raising your hand, putting yourself out there, and not being afraid to fail. When you move forward, even imperfectly, you position yourself to receive the opportunities life has to offer.

Identify one small action you can take today

toward your goals. It doesn't have to be perfect or grand—just get started. The more consistent you are, the more opportunities will come your way.

CREATING YOUR OWN LUCK

Luck isn't some magical force reserved for a select few. It's something you have the power to create through your mindset, actions, and persistence.

The more you prepare, the more you believe in your own potential, and the more you push through challenges, the luckier you'll become.

Instead of waiting for luck to find you, start building it yourself. Be bold. Be persistent. Stay open to new opportunities, and take action even when it's uncomfortable.

The "luckiest" people are the ones who understand that they are the architects of their own destiny. So go ahead, create your own luck, and watch your life transform in ways you never imagined.

REFLECTION QUESTIONS

1. When have you been "lucky" in the past? What preparation or action led to that luck?
2. What opportunities might you be missing because you're focused on a specific outcome?
3. How could you position yourself in environments where more opportunities

exist?
4. What action could you take today that might create future "luck"?

ACTION STEPS

1. Skill inventory: List your top 5 skills. Rate your proficiency. Choose one to deliberately improve this month—that's creating future luck.
2. Increase your surface area for luck: Attend one new event, join one new community, or reach out to one new person this week.
3. Document your "luck": For 30 days, write down every opportunity, connection, or fortunate circumstance. You'll see patterns in what creates them.
4. Take one bold action: Do something this week that increases your visibility or puts you in a new environment. Create opportunity through action.

25. FOLLOW THE PERSON WHO KNOWS THE WAY

"A wise person follows someone who knows the way."
— *Nigerian Proverb*

This Nigerian proverb captures a timeless truth about success, growth, and mastery. The journey to any meaningful goal is rarely a solo endeavor. Instead, it's a path best traveled by following those who have already navigated it—those whose proven results light the way forward.

Wisdom lies in recognizing that you don't need to forge a new trail when a reliable one already exists.

STANDING ON THE SHOULDERS OF GIANTS

This idea challenges the modern obsession with the "self-made" myth. We often imagine success as a solitary climb, a heroic battle against the odds. But the reality is humbler and more practical: no one succeeds alone.

Sir Isaac Newton, one of history's greatest minds, understood this when he wrote in a letter to Robert Hooke in 1675, "If I have seen further, it is by standing on the shoulders of Giants."

Newton's scientific breakthroughs—gravity, motion, calculus—were not conjured in isolation. They were built on the discoveries of predecessors like Galileo and Kepler. By following their paths, studying their work, and building on their insights, Newton reached heights that reshaped our understanding of the universe.

His humility reminds us that even the greatest achievements are collaborative, rooted in the wisdom of those who came before.

THE SHORTCUT TO MASTERY

The proverb and Newton's words share a common thread: success is a collective effort, a process of learning from those who've walked the path you aspire to tread.

Whether your goal is to build a thriving

career, improve your health, or cultivate stronger relationships, the journey is filled with obstacles—distractions, setbacks, and the weight of uncertainty.

Imagine trying to navigate a dense forest without a map or guide. You might eventually find your way, but at what cost? Days, months, or years of wandering?

The wise person, as the proverb suggests, doesn't waste time hacking through the underbrush. They find someone who knows the way—a mentor, a role model, or even a body of work from someone who's been there—and they follow.

PROVEN RESULTS ARE YOUR COMPASS

This principle is at the heart of lasting change. Small, consistent actions lead to extraordinary results. But those actions don't emerge in a vacuum—they are often borrowed from others who've succeeded.

Take fitness, for example. If you want to run a marathon, you find a proven plan from a seasoned runner—someone who's crossed the finish line—and follow their system: the weekly mileage, the recovery days, the nutrition. Their success becomes your blueprint.

Over time, with each step, you make their path your own. The same applies to any pursuit:

Want to grow a business? Study the habits

of entrepreneurs who've built companies that endure.

Want to write a book? Learn from authors who've published works you admire.

Want to live with more purpose? Observe the daily routines of those who radiate meaning and joy.

The key is to focus on proven results. Don't follow someone because they're loud or charismatic—follow them because their outcomes align with your aspirations.

ADAPTATION, NOT IMITATION

Like Newton standing on the shoulders of giants, you're leveraging their success to see further. This approach isn't about copying someone else's life or losing your uniqueness. It's about adopting systems that work.

When you follow someone who knows the way, you're not mimicking their every move; you're learning their principles, adapting their strategies, and applying them to your own journey.

The wise person knows that success isn't about being the first to blaze a trail—it's about reaching the destination efficiently and effectively.

FINDING YOUR GUIDES

So, how do you find these guides? Start by defining the results you want. Be specific: What does success look like for you?

Then seek out those who've achieved it. They

might be in your life—a colleague, a coach, a friend—or they might be distant figures whose books, interviews, or work you can study.

Once you've found them, don't just admire their success; dissect it:

- What habits got them there?
- What decisions did they make consistently?
- What mistakes did they avoid or learn from?

Then, take one small step to emulate their approach. If they wake up early to prioritize deep work, try it for a week. If they invest in learning new skills, commit to a single course.

Small steps, rooted in proven systems, compound into remarkable outcomes.

FROM FOLLOWER TO GUIDE

The beauty of this proverb is its call to humility and action. Following someone who knows the way requires setting aside ego—the temptation to "go it alone"—and embracing the discipline of learning.

It's not always glamorous. It might mean reading a book instead of scrolling social media, asking for feedback instead of assuming you're right, or sticking to a routine when you'd rather wing it.

But each step you take in the footsteps of a guide brings you closer to your goal.

And here's the deeper truth: following a guide doesn't make you a follower forever. As you learn, you internalize their wisdom. You adapt their map to your terrain. Eventually, you become the one who knows the way, lighting the path for others.

Just as Newton's discoveries became a foundation for future scientists, your progress can inspire those who follow. This is how progress compounds—not just for you, but for everyone who stands on your shoulders.

So, today, ask yourself: What's the next step on your journey? Who's already walked that path and left a trail of results you admire?

Find them. Study them. Follow their way. As the Nigerian proverb reminds us, wisdom isn't about forging a path alone—it's about having the courage to follow the right one.

One small step at a time, you'll stand on the shoulders of giants and see further than you ever imagined.

REFLECTION QUESTIONS

1. Who in your field has achieved the results you want? What do you know about their path?
2. What stops you from seeking out mentors or guides—pride, fear, or something else?
3. What's one specific system or habit from a successful person you could adopt this week?
4. Who followed a guide that helped them succeed, and what can you learn from their example?

ACTION STEPS

1. Identify three guides: List three people (living or dead, personal or public) who have achieved what you want to achieve.
2. Study their path: For one guide, spend 3 hours this week studying their journey—read their book, watch their interviews, analyze their strategies.
3. Adopt one system: Choose one specific practice, habit, or system from your guide and implement it for 30 days.
4. Seek mentorship: Reach out to one person in your field who's ahead of you. Ask for 15 minutes of their time to learn from their experience.

26. VISIBILITY AMPLIFIES VALUE

In the pursuit of your destiny, talent is only half the equation. The other half? Visibility. You can be the most skilled, innovative, or passionate person in the room, but if no one knows you're there, your value remains untapped. The truth is stark yet liberating: value that is not seen will not be recognized, received, or rewarded.

THE INVISIBLE GENIUS

Consider the countless brilliant minds who've toiled in obscurity—artists whose masterpieces gathered dust, thinkers whose ideas lay dormant, entrepreneurs whose businesses never took flight. Then look at those who've risen to the top, not always because they were the absolute best, but because they were the most visible. Visibility isn't a substitute for talent, but it's the spark that ignites its potential.

We've all been fed the narrative: work hard, keep your head down, and someone will notice. But the world doesn't work like that anymore—if it ever did.

Talent is essential, but it's not enough. The most successful people understand this. They don't wait for a spotlight; they build one.

History bears this out. Vincent van Gogh, now celebrated as a genius, sold only one painting in his lifetime. His brilliance was undeniable, but his visibility was near zero. Meanwhile, others with less raw talent but greater knack for self-promotion became household names in their own time.

The lesson? Your work may be extraordinary, but if it's hidden, it's as if it doesn't exist.

WHY VISIBILITY MATTERS

Visibility is the bridge between your value and the world's recognition of it. Here's why it's non-negotiable on your path to destiny:

Opportunity follows visibility. People can't hire you, collaborate with you, or champion you if they don't know you exist. Visibility puts you in the path of opportunity, opening doors you didn't even know were there.

Visibility builds trust. Familiarity breeds trust. The more people see you—your work, your ideas, your presence—the more they associate you with credibility and expertise. Repetition builds reputation.

Visibility increases perceived value. The more you're seen, the more your value is perceived. Think of brands that dominate your mind—not because they're always the best, but because they're everywhere. Your personal brand works the same way. Show up, and demand for your value will follow.

MAKING YOUR VALUE IMPOSSIBLE TO IGNORE

Your destiny demands that you step out of the shadows. Here's how to make your value impossible to ignore:

Claim your expertise. Stop waiting for permission to shine. Whether it's speaking up in a meeting, showcasing your work, or declaring your expertise, you are your own best advocate. Claim your place with confidence—because no one else will do it for you.

Leverage digital platforms. The digital age is your megaphone. Platforms like social media, blogs, or video channels let you share your voice with the world. Post consistently, share your insights, and engage with your audience. Every tweet, post, or video is a step toward greater visibility.

Be in the right rooms. Put yourself in the rooms where your audience gathers—whether it's industry conferences, online forums, or collaborative projects. Surround yourself with people who need your value. The right rooms lead to the right opportunities.

Show up consistently. Visibility isn't a one-off act; it's a habit. Show up day after day, even when it feels like no one's watching. Consistency compounds—over time, your presence becomes unforgettable.

Share your value generously. Don't hoard your expertise. Teach what you know, solve problems for others, and share your insights generously. When people see you as a source of solutions, they'll seek you out. Your value grows when it's shared.

THE FEAR OF VISIBILITY

Many talented people resist visibility because:

Fear of judgment: "What if people criticize me?" Imposter syndrome: "Who am I to put myself out there?" Perfectionism: "It's not good enough yet." Humility confusion: "Isn't self-promotion arrogant?"

But consider this: staying invisible isn't humility—it's hiding. And hiding your gifts doesn't serve anyone, least of all the people who need what you have to offer.

Visibility isn't arrogance when it's rooted in genuine value. It's responsibility. It's making sure that the people who need your contribution can find you.

STRATEGIC VISIBILITY

Not all visibility is equal. Strategic visibility means:

Being visible to the right people. Don't just chase numbers. Focus on being seen by the people who can benefit from your value or help you advance your mission.

Demonstrating value, not just presence. Every time you show up, offer something useful. Visibility without value is just noise.

Building a consistent brand. Your message, your aesthetic, your values—keep them consistent so people know what you stand for.

Choosing the right platforms. Be where your audience is. If they're on LinkedIn, be on LinkedIn. If they're at industry conferences, be at industry conferences.

THE COMPOUND EFFECT

The beautiful thing about visibility is that it compounds. Each time you show up, you:
- Reach new people who might not have found you otherwise
- Reinforce recognition with people who've seen you before
- Create more opportunities for collaboration and connection
- Build a body of work that demonstrates your expertise

- Increase the likelihood of being recommended or referred

The person who posts valuable content weekly for a year will have dramatically different opportunities than the person with equal talent who remains invisible.

REFLECTION QUESTIONS

1. On a scale of 1-10, how visible are you to the people who could benefit from your value?
2. What stops you from increasing your visibility—fear, perfectionism, or something else?
3. Where could you show up that would put you in front of your ideal audience?
4. What value could you share consistently that would make you impossible to ignore?

ACTION STEPS

1. Choose your platform: Identify the one platform where your ideal audience spends time. Commit to posting valuable content there twice weekly for 90 days.
2. Create a visibility plan: Schedule 10 specific visibility actions this month (posts, events, outreach, etc.). Put them in your calendar.

3. Share one piece of value today: Write a post, record a video, or share an insight that demonstrates your expertise. Do it today, not someday.
4. Track visibility metrics: For 30 days, track how many times you show up (posts, meetings, events). Watch the correlation between visibility and opportunity.

27. THE POWER OF CLOSING DOORS

We've been told that keeping our options open is wisdom, that flexibility equals freedom, that the more doors we leave ajar, the richer our lives become.

This is not true.

Here's the truth: every option you refuse to close is quietly draining your power.

THE COST OF OPEN OPTIONS

Think about it. Right now, you're probably keeping a dozen doors half-open. That business idea you might pursue someday. That career pivot you're considering. That project you'll start when the timing is perfect. That relationship you're keeping lukewarm just in case.

You tell yourself you're being smart, strategic,

open to opportunities. But what you're actually doing is spreading yourself so thin that you become translucent. You're building a mansion of maybes while the foundation of your actual life crumbles.

Every "I'll keep that option open" is a choice—a choice to not choose. And in that non-choice, you lose something precious: momentum, clarity, and the raw energy that comes from full commitment. Here's what nobody tells you about options: they're not free. Each one you maintain demands mental energy, emotional bandwidth, focus. That half-considered alternative career path isn't sitting quietly in the background. It's whispering to you during your current work. It's making you question whether you should really invest in this presentation, this relationship, this moment.

Those possibilities you're protecting? They're not opportunities waiting to bloom. They're distractions dressed in potential's clothing.

THE LIBERATION OF COMMITMENT

There's a strange magic that happens when you finally close a door and lock it. The moment you say "This is my path, and these are not," something shifts. The fog clears. The noise quiets. Suddenly, you can see the road ahead with stunning clarity because you're no longer glancing sideways every few steps.

Commitment isn't a prison—it's a liberation. When you choose one thing and eliminate the rest, you're not limiting yourself. You're unleashing yourself. You're taking all that scattered energy you were using to juggle possibilities and channeling it into a single, powerful direction.

The masters, the legends, the people who actually change the world—they're not the ones with the most options. They're the ones who burned their other options so completely that retreat became impossible and moving forward became inevitable.

THE PARALYSIS OF CHOICE

If you stand at a crossroads analyzing every possible outcome, calculating every probability, weighing every potential eventuality, you know what happens? Nothing.

You become a statue at an intersection, a monument of indecision, frozen by the weight of your own overthinking.

Success doesn't belong to those who make the perfect choice. It belongs to those who make a choice and then make it perfect through sheer force of will and commitment.

The finish line isn't waiting for the person with the best options. It's waiting for the person who picked a direction and refused to stop running.

YOUR CHALLENGE

So here's your challenge, your invitation, your wake-up call: What door are you going to close today?

What half-hearted maybe are you going to transform into a definitive no? What backup plan are you going to set on fire? What safety net are you going to cut away?

Pick your lane. Not the perfect lane, not the safest lane, not the lane that keeps all other lanes accessible. Pick YOUR lane—the one that makes your heart beat faster, the one that scares you just enough to make you feel alive.

And then stay there. When the road gets rough (and it will), when other lanes look smoother (and they will), when doubt creeps in (and it absolutely will)—stay in your lane. Dominate it. Make it yours so completely that people forget there were ever other options.

THE WISDOM OF ELIMINATION

The world will tell you to hedge your bets, to keep your options open, to never fully commit. The world is also full of people who never finish anything, who never master anything, who spend their entire lives at the starting line, eternally ready to begin but never actually beginning.

You're better than that. You're capable of more than perpetual preparation.

Choose one thing. Pour everything into it. Let the other options die. Not because they weren't good, but because you only have one life, and trying to live all possible versions of it means you never truly live any of them.

Cut the noise. Close the doors. Commit completely. Choose one thing. Go all in. And win.

REFLECTION QUESTIONS

1. What doors are you keeping half-open that are draining your energy?
2. What would you achieve if you committed fully to one path for the next year?
3. What are you afraid of losing if you close certain doors?
4. What door, if closed, would give you the most clarity and focus?

ACTION STEPS

1. Inventory your open doors: List every project, possibility, or path you're keeping open. Be comprehensive.
2. Close three doors this week: Choose three options you're going to definitively eliminate. Write them down and commit to not reconsidering them.
3. Double down on one: Identify your primary path. For the next 90 days, put 80% of your energy there and only 20% everywhere else.

4. Track the difference: Journal for 30 days about how closing doors affects your focus, energy, and progress. Notice the liberation.

28. THE UNVEILING OF YOUR NEXT LEVEL

There comes a pivotal moment in every journey—a profound realization that the very essence which propelled you to your current standing is not the force that will carry you to the extraordinary vistas you envision.

This is not a judgment of your past, but a clarion call to your future. The version of you that has meticulously navigated the paths thus far, while commendable, is merely the foundation upon which your grandest aspirations must be built.

WHAT GOT YOU HERE WON'T GET YOU THERE

To truly ascend, to reach those towering peaks of ambition and fulfillment, demands an evolution—a courageous shedding of the familiar for the magnificent unknown.

Consider this: monumental goals are not merely extensions of your present reality; they are invitations to new heights of being. And these new heights, by their very nature, necessitate a profound shift in perspective. They demand new thinking, a liberation from the confines of old paradigms, and the establishment of new, elevated standards for yourself.

This is where the magic begins, for new standards are the fertile ground from which a new you—a more potent and capable version of yourself—will inevitably emerge.

It is a fundamental truth that the echoes of yesterday's habits and the grooves of yesterday's thinking cannot, by any stretch of imagination, sculpt the vibrant realities of tomorrow.

YOUR CAPACITY FOR TRANSFORMATION

To cling to the familiar is to condemn yourself to a perpetual cycle of the same results. But within you resides a boundless capacity for transformation.

You possess the innate power to not only achieve audacious new goals but to fundamentally reshape the very fabric of your existence. You are capable of becoming the most authentic, powerful, and radiant version of yourself, being truly aligned with your deepest desires.

Your dreams are not distant fantasies; they are blueprints for your becoming. The first step on this transformative odyssey is to clearly articulate what it is you truly desire. Let your aspirations be vivid, tangible, and deeply resonant with your soul.

Once this clarity is achieved, the next, equally crucial step is to understand, with unwavering honesty, who you need to become to manifest these desires. This is not about imitation, but about internalizing the qualities, the mindset, and the very spirit of the person who effortlessly achieves what you seek.

THE COMMITMENT TO BECOMING

This journey demands an unwavering commitment, a fierce dedication to making the impossible, possible. You must cultivate the person capable of making this happen, brick by brick, belief by belief.

This involves the deliberate construction of empowering beliefs that serve as the bedrock of your new reality. It means forging new habits that align with your elevated standards, and embodying behaviors that reflect the person you are becoming.

It requires the acquisition of new skillsets, honing

your craft, and expanding your capabilities. Furthermore, it calls for the development of sophisticated mental models, frameworks for understanding and interacting with the world that empower you to navigate challenges and seize opportunities.

And crucially, it involves the conscious cultivation of relationships that uplift, inspire, and actively contribute to your ascent.

THE PRUNING REQUIRED

Just as growth requires nourishment, it also demands pruning. To make space for the magnificent person you are destined to become, you must courageously identify and sever ties with the beliefs, habits, people, and behaviors that are no longer serving your highest good.

This may mean walking away from relationships, even those long-held, that subtly or overtly diminish your spirit or impede your progress. This act of liberation is not abandonment; it is an act of profound self-love, creating the necessary void for your true self to expand and flourish.

YOUR TRANSFORMATION PLAN

With this newfound clarity and commitment, the path forward becomes illuminated:

Make new plans, audacious and inspiring, that reflect your evolved vision.

Set your goals not as mere tasks, but as

declarations of your becoming.

Figure out, with unwavering resolve, the person you need to embody to achieve these goals.

Then, with every fiber of your being, commit to doing whatever it takes to become that person.

Embrace the discomfort of growth, the exhilaration of challenge, and the profound satisfaction of self-mastery.

As you embark on this courageous journey of self-reinvention, you will not only begin to produce the results you desire, but you will discover a strength and resilience within you that you never knew existed.

Trust the process, trust yourself. You will be fine; you will be fine.

REFLECTION QUESTIONS

1. What version of yourself got you to where you are today?
2. What version of yourself do you need to become to reach your next goal?
3. What beliefs, habits, or relationships do you need to release to make room for your evolution?
4. What new standards do you need to set for yourself?

ACTION STEPS

1. Define your future self: Write a detailed

description of the person you need to become to achieve your biggest goal. Include their habits, beliefs, standards, and relationships.
2. Identify the gap: List the specific differences between current you and future you. Be brutally honest about what needs to change.
3. Choose one evolution: Pick one habit, belief, or behavior to change this month that brings you closer to your future self.
4. Track your transformation: Daily, rate yourself 1-10 on how well you showed up as your future self. Watch the score climb.

END OF PART FIVE

You now have practical wisdom for accelerating your journey: creating luck through preparation and action, following proven mentors, making your value visible, closing doors to create focus, and continuously evolving into the person your destiny requires.

In Part Six, you'll read my personal testimony of how these principles worked in my own life—proof that what I'm teaching you isn't theory, but lived reality.

PART SIX: A PERSONAL TESTIMONY

29. WRITING MY FIRST BOOK

I had always had this dream of being a writer. From as early as I can remember, I read anything I could lay my hands on: comics, magazines, novels, books, newspapers, the Bible. Anything I could read was game. Thanks to the books my mom and dad were gracious enough to bring into our home. My dad was also an avid reader of books and magazines like Time magazine. This was the foundation for my voracious appetite for information and knowledge.

THE FOUNDATION OF A DREAM

From the age of 10, I focused on reading novels. I read huge, monstrous novels that seemed too big for my age and my head. I remember in secondary school, my friends spent their money buying clothes and shoes. I spent my money on books.

If a thief rummaged through my suitcase, he would be totally disappointed because all he would find would be books and drab clothes. I had very little interest in fashion, although that changed after I realized the importance of looking good in attracting members of the opposite sex!

All those books I read and the millions of words I devoured began to percolate in my young mind, and I began to see myself as a writer. I tried my hands on writing short stories, but nothing ever came out of it. A short course in writing at the age of 17 laid the foundation for the next 4 decades of my life. It gave me the tools I needed to put my ideas on paper, although that didn't happen until about 10 years later.

THE UNIVERSITY MISADVENTURE

I had a mis-adventure in the university, having no idea why I was there. I kind of floated through the system until I decided to set myself free before it drove me completely crazy. One day, I got up and left without a degree.

I can talk about it now, but back then, I felt so much pain because I didn't have a degree. Thank God for guys like Bill Gates, Steve Jobs, Michael Dell, Richard Branson, and very recently, Mark Zuckerberg who redeemed the image of restless, entrepreneurial, leave-school-before-degree types like me.

All I ever wanted to do was write and speak to large groups of people. The university gave me no direction toward my goal. I wish I knew someone like me, someone who could talk to me and give me clarity; someone who could show me the power of my talent, and set me on a course of self-actualization and success.

But alas, I was alone. There was no one to give me guidance.

THE MUSIC DETOUR

As I went along, I began to use one of my skillsets: singing. I sang in so many Churches that I lost count. I made a living through music.

But somewhere in my soul, the words I had ingested for years just wouldn't let me rest. They demanded expression, and I discovered that singing couldn't bring me to my destiny. Then I decided to write a book.

That was the beginning of change in my life.

THAT FATEFUL DAY

Like I said in the opening words of this chapter, my first book was tough. I had never done it before. All I had was my singing skill and my gift of words.

I will never forget the day the landlady of the one bedroom flat I lived in showed up and found me at home writing.

"What are you doing at home at this hour of the day?" she asked.

"I am writing, working on a book," I replied.
"You are writing? Writing what?" she laughed with derision. "Why don't you get a job like everybody else and stop deceiving yourself that you are a writer?"

I was shattered, devastated by her words. I felt shame. I felt the old pain resurrecting from within, haunting me again. But I summoned the strength to ignore her and kept writing because I had no choice.

I was broke. I was desperate. And my only hope for survival was the completion of that book. If I didn't complete it, I was sure to starve or experience some form of pain worse than starvation.

THE TRANSFORMATION

I completed that book and it sold like crazy. That book freed me from the tyranny of a job. It freed me from poverty. It freed me from the tyranny of crooked men in religious disguise who wanted to exploit my singing ability for self-aggrandizement. It freed me to live my dream.

One thing that made the difference for me was my ability to sell. I learned to sell to survive. My skillsets served me well when I released my first book. I went to places no writer had gone before. I was not ashamed to talk to people about my product, so I sold like crazy.

When I tell people that I am a writer, some of them

look at me like I am crazy until I tell them how many books I have sold. Some of them still don't get it, until I put it in figures, then their eyes light up like a Christmas tree!

I write, I sell, I make enough money to live a good life, and I do it effortlessly.

THE FLOODGATES OPEN

After my first successful book, other books found expression through me: *Action*, *Releasing The Success Within*. Then I wrote *Rules For Single Ladies*. After that, it seemed as if I tapped into an ocean of wisdom. The ideas just kept on coming. It was effortless. I had found the fountain of Grace.

Over 60 books later, I am still writing. The dream of that 17-year-old writer has come to pass and has surpassed all my expectations because I stayed true to my calling.

Because of my tenacity, you are reading this book, *A Thousand Ways To Your Destiny*.

WHY I KEEP WRITING

Why do I keep writing? Simple.

It thrills my soul when a man walks up to me and says, "I read your books since I was a teenager and it has made the difference in my life." I feel honored when a lady walks up to me and says, "8 years ago, I started reading your books and today I am married with children. Thanks."

Writing these words brings tears of gratitude to

my eyes. I am grateful to the Lord for using my talent to change lives, to be a blessing to millions of people in different parts of the world. I can't imagine where I would have been if it weren't for the gentle guidance of the Holy Spirit and the Mercies of the Lord Jesus Christ who kept me on the right path.

To all who have bought and read my books, to all who have attended my seminars and programs, I am eternally grateful for honoring me, for honoring my talents by allowing me to be a part of your life, a part of your journey, your history, and a part of your destiny.

You are the reason I do what I do. I make a commitment to stay true to my calling, to my talents, to my path, and to be a blessing to all those to whom the Lord would grant me access.

THE LESSONS IN MY STORY

Now that you know my story, let me tell you what it proves about everything I've taught you in this book:

There truly are a thousand ways to your destiny. When the university path didn't work, I found the music path. When music wasn't my ultimate destination, I found the writing path. When traditional publishing wasn't available, I found self-publishing. Each closed door led to an open one.

You must proceed with uncertainty. I had no

guarantee that book would sell. I had never done it before. I had no publisher, no distribution, no marketing budget. I just had words and desperation. I proceeded anyway.

Fear will try to paralyze you. That landlady's mockery could have stopped me. The pain of not having a degree could have convinced me I wasn't qualified. The fear of poverty could have sent me scrambling for a "safe" job. But I rebelled against that fear through daily action.

Don't wait for permission or perfect conditions. I didn't wait for someone to validate my dream or for circumstances to be ideal. I wrote in a one-bedroom flat while broke. I sold books in ways no one else was doing. I created my own path.

Authenticity attracts your tribe. I wrote what was real to me, what I actually believed. And that authenticity connected with people who needed exactly what I had to offer. Over 60 books later, those connections have become a movement.

Visibility amplifies value. I wasn't ashamed to sell my book. I went where other writers hadn't gone. I made my work visible. And visibility created opportunity.

Your past doesn't determine your future. No degree? Didn't matter. No traditional path? Didn't matter. No connections? Didn't matter. I created value, and value always finds recognition.

WHAT THIS MEANS FOR YOU

If with no connections, no money, and no traditional credentials, I could build a life and career through writing; if I could find my thousand ways despite closed doors and mockery and uncertainty...

Then you can find yours.

Your circumstances might be different. Your dream might be different. Your path will certainly be different. But the principles are the same:

There are a thousand ways to your destiny. You don't need to see them all. You just need to see the next step and take it. You need to proceed despite uncertainty. You need to rebel against fear through daily action. You need to be authentic and visible. You need to trust that when one door closes, another opens.

MY PRAYER FOR YOU

I pray that you experience what I experienced: the liberation of living your calling, the joy of seeing your work impact lives, the financial freedom that comes from creating value, the peace of knowing you're walking in your purpose.

I pray that you find your thousand ways. I pray that when people mock your dreams, you remember my landlady and keep working anyway. I pray that when doors close, you remember that I've stood where you're standing, and those closed doors led to open ones.

I pray that years from now, you'll write your

own testimony of how you found your way, and someone else will read it and find courage to pursue theirs.

This isn't just my story. This is proof that the principles in this book work. This is evidence that there truly are a thousand ways.

Now go find yours.

REFLECTION QUESTIONS

1. What part of my story resonates most with your current situation?
2. What closed door in your life could actually be redirecting you toward your real path?
3. What mockery or discouragement are you letting stop you?
4. If I could proceed with uncertainty and succeed, what's your excuse?

ACTION STEPS

1. Write your future testimony: Write the story of your success as if it's already happened. Include the obstacles you overcame and how you found your way.
2. Identify your first book moment: What's the equivalent of "writing my first book" for you? What's the thing you need to create despite uncertainty?
3. Find your selling strategy: Like I learned

to sell books, what do you need to learn to make your dream viable? Take one step toward learning it this week.
4. Start before you're ready: Don't wait for perfect conditions. Start your version of "writing in a one-bedroom flat" today.

A FINAL WORD TO YOU

Thank you for reading this book. Thank you for investing your time, your money, and your attention in these pages. I don't take that lightly.

My deepest hope is that something in these words has shifted something in you. That you now see possibilities where you once saw only dead ends. That you now believe in your thousand ways where you once believed in only one blocked path.

But more than that, I hope you act. Because this book is worthless if it's just good ideas that never leave these pages. This book only has value if it propels you into motion, into courage, into your destiny.

So go. Find your way. Knock on your doors. Create your value. Be visible. Close unnecessary doors. Evolve into who you need to become.

And when you succeed—and you will—remember to light the way for someone else. Just as I'm attempting to do for you.

Your thousand ways are waiting. Now go claim

them.
With all my belief in your potential,
Praise George, January 2026, Milton Keynes, United kingdom.

30. CONCLUSION: YOUR THOUSAND WAYS AWAIT

We've reached the end of our journey together through these pages, but the real journey—your journey—is just beginning.

Let me bring you back to where we started, to that one-bedroom flat where my landlady laughed at my dreams. Where I sat with my fingers on a keyboard, broke and desperate, with nothing but words and hope. Where the conventional path had rejected me, and I had to find another way.

That moment crystallized everything I've shared

with you in this book: there are a thousand ways to your destiny.

WHAT YOU'VE DISCOVERED

Through these chapters, you've learned to:

Break free from limiting beliefs that told you there was only one path, that made you beg instead of create, that kept you enslaved to situations that no longer serve you, that convinced you to wait for fate instead of making things happen, and that taught you to fear failure instead of learning from it.

Understand your unique journey—recognizing that your path will have a thousand variations, that companions will come and go, that you must walk authentically even when it's unconventional, that you're not limited by geography or circumstance, and that divine redirection often looks like loss before it reveals itself as blessing.

Take massive action despite uncertainty, knowing when to persist and when to pivot, knocking on doors instead of waiting for invitations, understanding the protocols for accessing new levels, and trusting that the next step will reveal itself as you walk.

Master your inner game by refusing to compare yourself to others, showing up authentically instead of performing, protecting your privacy and energy, rebelling against fear through daily action, and reframing your relationship with scarcity.

Apply practical wisdom by creating your own luck through preparation, following proven mentors, making your value visible, knowing when to close doors to create focus, and continuously evolving into the person your destiny requires.

You've read my story of writing that first book and how it transformed everything. But now it's time for your story.

THE QUESTION THAT MATTERS

As you close this book, there's only one question that matters:

What will you do with what you now know?

Will you return to the comfortable cage of "one path" thinking? Will you go back to begging people who don't value you? Will you stay in environments that drain you because at least they're familiar? Will you wait for certainty before you act? Will you let fear paralyze you?

Or will you remember that there are a thousand ways to your destiny?

THE TRUTH ABOUT YOUR THOUSAND WAYS

Here's what I need you to understand: those thousand ways aren't theoretical. They're not metaphorical. They're real, tangible, available

paths that exist right now.
But here's the catch: you only discover them by moving.
You don't see the thousand ways by standing still, analyzing, overthinking, waiting for perfect clarity. You see them by taking a step. By knocking on a door. By trying something new. By walking away from what no longer serves you. By acting despite uncertainty.
Each action you take reveals new possibilities. Each door you knock on shows you two more doors you didn't see before. Each step forward illuminates more of the path. Each person you meet connects you to three more people. Each skill you develop opens five new opportunities.
The thousand ways aren't waiting for you to discover them. They're waiting for you to create them through movement, action, courage, and faith.

YOUR DESTINY IS NOT A MAYBE

Before we part, I need you to internalize something I said at the beginning:
There's greatness in you. You will manifest your greatness. You will live an awesome life—an enviable life, a life worthy of emulation. Greatness is your birthright.
This isn't motivational fluff. This isn't positive thinking nonsense. This is truth.

You were born with everything you need to live a great life. The resources are within you. The capacity is within you. The potential is within you. Living your greatness is not a matter of if. It's a matter of making a decision to live like you were born to live.

It doesn't matter where you are right now. It doesn't matter what challenges you face. It doesn't matter how messed up your life looks at this moment.

What matters is the decision you make right now, as you read these words, about who you will be and what you will do going forward.

THE CHOICE BEFORE YOU

You're standing at a crossroads. You've been here before, but this time is different. This time you have new eyes. This time you see beyond the illusion of "one way."

You can choose to:

Stay where you are, doing what you've always done, getting what you've always gotten. The familiar path of mediocrity, the comfortable cage of "at least I have this."

Or you can choose to:

Step into your greatness. Find one of your thousand ways. Knock on a door. Take a leap. Walk away from what no longer serves you. Create value. Make yourself visible. Follow a mentor. Act despite fear. Proceed with uncertainty. Trust the unfolding.

The choice is yours. It's always been yours.

WHAT I WANT FOR YOU

I want you to experience what I experienced when that first book sold—not just the financial freedom, but the psychological liberation of knowing: "I can create my own opportunities. I'm not dependent on anyone's approval. There are a thousand ways, and I just found one of them."

I want you to feel the power of walking away from a toxic environment and discovering that not only do you survive, you thrive.

I want you to experience the confidence that comes from knocking on doors that others said would never open, and watching them swing wide.

I want you to know the joy of meeting strangers who become strategic partners because you were visible, because you offered value, because you were moving toward your destiny and they were moving toward theirs and your paths intersected at exactly the right moment.

I want you to taste the freedom of living authentically, not performing for approval, not begging for acceptance, not shrinking yourself to fit into spaces that were never designed for you.

I want you to discover that when you're on the right path, things flow. Not because success is easy, but because you're aligned with your purpose, operating in your strengths, surrounded by people who recognize your value.

THE BEGINNING, NOT THE END

This conclusion is not an ending. It's a beginning.

Everything you've read prepares you for what comes next: the actual living of your life with new awareness, new courage, new wisdom.

The principles in this book aren't theoretical. They're practical, tested, proven. I've lived them. Countless others have lived them. Now it's your turn.

YOUR NEXT STEP

You know what you need to do. You've known it for a while now, maybe even before you picked up this book. That thing you've been avoiding, that change you've been postponing, that dream you've been dismissing, that door you've been afraid to knock on, that environment you've been afraid to leave.

You know.

So here's what I want you to do right now, before you close this book:

Write down one action. Just one. One concrete step you will take in the next 24 hours toward one of your thousand ways.

Not someday. Not when you're ready. Not when the conditions are perfect.

Tomorrow. Within 24 hours.

Write it here:
Within 24 hours, I will:
_____

That's your starting point. That's your first step on one of your thousand ways.

THE PROMISE

I can't promise that your first step will lead directly to success. I can't promise that the first door you knock on will open. I can't promise that the first path you try will be the right one.

But I can promise this: if you keep moving, you will find your way.

If you keep knocking, doors will open. If you keep creating value, people will recognize it. If you keep walking away from what doesn't serve you, you'll find what does. If you keep acting despite fear, courage will become your nature. If you keep proceeding despite uncertainty, clarity will emerge.

The thousand ways exist. They're real. They're available. They're waiting.

But they're waiting for you to move.

A FINAL WORD

Years from now, when you're living the life you once only dreamed about, when you're walking in your purpose with confidence and joy, when you're surrounded by people who value you, in environments that celebrate you, doing work that fulfills you, remember this moment.

Remember that there was a time when you thought there was only one way, and that way was blocked. Remember that you felt stuck, trapped, limited.

And remember that everything changed when you realized: there are a thousand ways to your destiny. The way you chose might not have been the way anyone else would have chosen. It might not have looked like what you expected. It might have twisted and turned and surprised you at every corner.

But it was your way. One of your thousand ways. And it brought you home to yourself.

GO FORTH

There are a thousand ways to your destiny.
Stop acting like there's only one.
Stop begging. Stop waiting. Stop shrinking. Stop playing small.
Find your way. Walk your path. Knock on your doors. Create your value. Show up authentically. Act courageously.
Your greatness is waiting.
Your destiny is calling.
Your thousand ways are open before you.
Now go.

Remember: Every expert was once a beginner. Every master was once a student. Every success

story started with a single step.
This is your moment. This is your time. This is your beginning.
There are a thousand ways to your destiny.
Choose one, and start walking.
I'll see you at the top.

ABOUT THE AUTHOR

Praise George

PRAISE GEORGE is the author of over 60 books that have impacted millions of readers across multiple continents. After leaving university without a degree, he defied conventional wisdom by pursuing his dream of becoming a writer despite having  no credentials, no connections, and no money. His first self-published book became a bestseller, launching a three-decade career in writing, speaking, and mentoring.

His works span personal development, relationships, faith, and success principles. He is known for his raw authenticity, practical wisdom, and ability to blend spiritual insight with actionable strategies. His books have been particularly transformative for young professionals, entrepreneurs, and anyone navigating major life transitions.

He is the bestselling author of several books including:
Move In Silence, Finding Direction, Start With What You Have From Where
You Are, Success Habits, The Gift Of Work, Business Success and Clarity.

He continues to write prolifically, speaking at conferences and churches, and mentoring emerging writers and leaders. He lives in the UK with his wife.

To have Praise George as a speaker at your event, please contact:
Praise George,
E-mail: praise@praisegeorge.org

Connect with me on social media:
Facebook: @praisegeorge
Twitter:@praisegeorge
Instagram:@praisegeorge
TikTok: @realpraisegeorge

Grab my books at: https://youwillbefine.org

BOOKS BY THIS AUTHOR

Move In Silence.

The parrot is always talking, always chatting. It cannot keep its mouth shut. The parrot is shut up in a cage and people use it as a source of entertainment.

The eagle is without speech, but it flies freely and dominates the sky.

Some people are like parrots. They are talkative, they keep chattering, telling everyone everything, exposing their plans, their goals, their next big move. They tell people their secrets thereby placing themselves in the hands of their enemies and people who hate them. When you tell people your plans you give them information which becomes ammunition in their hands to attack and destroy you. But these people wonder why their plans keep failing and their goals do not become a reality. They don't understand that they are behind their own misfortune, they are the ones orchestrating their own calamity, they are the malevolent power behind their own ruin.

They don't understand that every misfortune in their life is as a result of something they said, something they told someone; a secret divulged, a plan uncovered. They don't understand that the more they keep telling people about their plans, the more they will be attacked and sabotaged by envious and evil people who will never be happy to see them successful and make progress in life.

But they never make the connection between their senseless chattering and their misfortunes and near misses at success. They never hold themselves accountable for ruining their own opportunities, ruining their own chances and ruining their own lives. They blame everybody else but themselves. But like the talkative parrot, they will remain locked in a cage of mediocrity, poverty and failure until they learn to keep silent like the eagle and soar.

The eagle is the opposite of the parrot. It doesn't chatter carelessly like the parrot. It keeps its mouth shut, focuses on its objectives, spreads its wings, soars and dominates the sky. Be like the eagle. Stop telling everyone what you want to do, what you want to accomplish, what you want to own and possess. Keep your mouth shut. Keep your plans private. Do the necessary work that life demands of you and manifest your goals by creating and delivering great value.

Stop chattering like a parrot.

Keep your plans private. Move in silence and soar like the eagle.

Do the work. Get the results.

Do the work. Accomplish great things.

Do the work. Transform your skill sets into value delivering tools.

Do the work. Create and deliver value which attract great rewards into your life.

BOOKS BY THIS AUTHOR

Finding Direction

Finding Direction.

Life is a journey. We want to know what to do next on our journey. We want to be sure that we are going in the right direction in life. The Lord wants to guide us, he wants to show us what to do, where to go. He wants us to live in the very centre of his will for our lives. The centre of his will is where we find peace, provision and protection.
When we follow the Lord's direction, we will manifest our assignment effortlessly.

BOOKS BY THIS AUTHOR

Life On Your Own Terms.

You were given a life. You have a time frame to live this life. You have certain talents and abilities to help you live your life according to an assignment which has been coded into your soul. This is your life. It is not an audition. It is not a trial run. It is the real thing. You are not going to get another chance at it. This is all you've got. This is all you will ever have. Give it your best shot. Live life the way you want to live it. Live it the way you envisioned it in your mind. Live it the way you want. Live it for yourself. Yes, the meaning of life is found in your contribution to other people, is about you employing your skillsets to create value, to make a difference, to change the world. But you determine your contribution, you determine who you make a contribution to, where you make that contribution, how you make that contribution and when you make that contribution.
This is it.

This book will show you how to live your life on your own terms. Not on the terms of your friends, not on the terms of society, not on the terms of your haters.
No.
On your own terms.
You are the driver in the driver's seat of your own life. You determine the direction of your life. You determine the direction and speed of your life. And yes, you take full responsibility for your outcomes.

BOOKS BY THIS AUTHOR

Success Habits.

Why are some people successful, achieve their goals, fulfil their dreams, while others struggle throughout their lives with little or no positive accomplishment or results to show for their existence? Why do certain people produce exceptional results and dominate in their chosen fields of endeavour while some others crawl shamefully through life? Why do some people create wealth from thin air while some others are perpetually in debt and penury? What do all successful people have in common? What do all achievers have in common? The answer is in their habits.

A habit is a course of behaviour. It is acting in a particular manner consistently. A habit is something you have become accustomed to. It is not a chance behaviour, neither is it something you do by accident. It is something you do often, frequently, daily or as the occasion to act in such a manner necessitates or demands. A habit is an ingrained pattern of behaviour in a person. It is part of your being, your personality. It is something you do without thinking. It is who you are. The principle of success is be, do, have. Who you are determines what you do and will ultimately determine the quality of outcomes you have in your life. Your outcomes are a product of who you are. Trying to produce different results without first changing who you are is the definition of insanity. Success is the outcome of a positive habit. Failure is the outcome of a negative habit. Whether we realise it or not, our habits are taking us in the direction of an inevitable conclusion of either success or failure. Peter Drucker said, "The very best way to predict the future is to create it." Our habits not only predict but also create our future.

Our habits program us for either success or failure. When you imbibe a new and positive habit, it sets you on the path of success. Opportunities materialise in your life because of the person you have become. If more people discover this vital success secret, they will stop running around in panic, without direction, seeking miracles. They will settle down to the task of developing their innate abilities. The secret of success and wealth is in who you are. Because it is in who you are, nobody can give it to you or take it away from you.

You are the secret to your own greatness, the instrument of your own breakthrough, the key to your own miracle. God gave us the power to predict, determine and create our future by our habits.

Successful people all over the world produce positive outcomes because of their positive habits. Their results are predictable because their habits are predictable. As you begin to practice what successful people do, you will imbibe positive habits and start producing predictable results. Success is not an accident. It is a conscious and deliberate process of impressing your dreams on reality. It is asserting yourself in the world's market place and producing powerful, predictable results through your positive habits. Enjoy!

BOOKS BY THIS AUTHOR

Clarity

Clarity is the ability to know what to do to get you from where you are to where you want to be in life. It is knowing the next step to take on your journey. Some people are stagnated and confused in life because they do not see beyond where they are presently on their journey. They are confined to the limits of their environment and circumstances, they are limited to their past accomplishments and achievements, they are chained down to the successes of yesterday while they have absolutely no idea how to move their lives forward today. Clarity helps you see beyond the limitations of your circumstances and environment to see the possibilities that exist around you but you don't even realise. Clarity gives you the strategic tools to move your life forward in the direction of your dream and shows you how to get what you want in life.

BOOKS BY THIS AUTHOR

The Laws Of Attraction.

What makes a lady become irresistibly attractive to a man to make him develop burning desire to do almost anything to be with her?

What magnetizes a man to a woman and captivates his heart, will and emotions? What makes a man want to date a lady enter into courtship with her and get married to her?

What does a lady do to make a man want to forsake all others and FOCUS on her alone?

What makes a man want to be with that lady, spend time with her, desperately want to put that ring on her finger and be faithful to her for the rest of his life?

What makes a man unable to get a lady off his mind no matter how hard other ladies try to seduce him away from this special lady?

What makes a man try to to impress a lady with expensive gifts, money and other material enticements?

How does a lady become the object of a man's dream and waking thoughts?

How does a lady attract the man of her dreams and keep him committed to her?

The Laws Of Attraction will give you the answers to these questions and answers to many other questions in your mind. This book will show you how to attract quality people into your life. You will learn how to become a positive influence at work, at business and in your community.
You will develop and master the skills to make you become irresistible.

Printed in Dunstable, United Kingdom